Grow Old Along with Me

Grow Old Along with Me

Lorna Cruddas

ISIS
LARGE PRINT
Oxford

First published in Great Britain 2007
by
ISIS Publishing Ltd

Published in Large Print 2007 by ISIS Publishing Ltd.,
7 Centremead, Osney Mead, Oxford OX2 0ES
by arrangement with
the Author

British Library Cataloguing in Publication Data
Cruddas, Lorna
    Grow old along with me. – Large print ed.
    (Isis reminiscence series)
    1. Cruddas, Len
    2. Cruddas, Lorna
    3. Inventors – England – Biography
    4. Large type books
    I. Title
    942'.085'092

ISBN 978–0–7531–9446–1 (hb)
ISBN 978–0–7531–9447–8 (pb)

Printed and bound in Great Britain by
T. J. International Ltd., Padstow, Cornwall

We've written my life story because Lorna was fascinated by my tales of growing up in Yorkshire and the West Midlands. This account is really the expression of the love we've found and the fun we've experienced together.

We'd like to dedicate it, with our love, to our families, and to those of our loved ones who've gone before us, but who are for ever in our hearts.

CHAPTER
ONE

The message was brief and to the point, "You'll have to fetch Len back, before the lad gets hisself killed". It had come from Grandma, who had been looking after me. I'd been sent to stay with my maternal grandmother when Laurie, my younger brother, decided to make a hurried entrance into the world. He had been born as Mother was coming down the stairs. Father had grabbed him, placed Mother and the new baby on a chair, and run next door for help. The year was 1931, and I was two years old at the time. I suppose my parents would have been pleased to have me out of their way for a while, but my unfortunate fascination with delivery horses put paid to that. In those days, horse and cart made many deliveries. My favourite was the milkman; I can see the trap now, with its two milk churns leaving just enough room for the milkman to stand in between. The lady of the house would come to the side of the cart, and ask for a pint or two, or perhaps a gill (a quarter of a pint), and hand her jug to the milkman. He'd dip his measure into the churn, and pour the milk into her jug. "Come on, my old beauty," he would say to his pony, and with no more ado, off the pony would amble to the next house. Apparently, I had no fear of these animals, and would go running out of Grandma's house, to stand under the bellies of the horses. My poor Grandma couldn't cope with this, and instead of me making a month's visit so my mother could have a break, I had to be taken home again.

My home was in Goole, East Yorkshire, and my parents were Elizabeth Jackson (or Bess as my father called her) and Robert Cruddas. Bess had been brought up mainly by her maternal grandparents, Hannah and Harry Fussey in Hull, and lived with them until she was nine. On Sundays, she loved to go to the greengrocery warehouse with her grandfather to feed the cats. Her grandmother would put some milk into a bottle and give them some boiled fish to take. They would then go down to the slipway on the river opposite Immingham Docks to watch the great dray horses having their "feathers" washed.

Her mother Elizabeth was a nurse and was always busy and her father Edward was in the British Army in India for most of her early years. He returned briefly to England before embarking for Europe to fight in the First World War. He was wounded and taken prisoner in 1915 and on his release he was discharged with a gratuity of five hundred pounds. He used this to purchase a small shop, with greengrocery on one side and sweets and tobacco on the other. My mother returned to live with her parents above the shop. Her father smoked, shouted and bullied and she hated him. My grandmother worked with him, and did the ordering. Each morning my grandmother and Bess would get up early to fetch the handcart to collect the vegetables. They had two more girls, Marian born when Mum was nine and Joyce when she was fourteen, but Mother lost touch with them during the war. Their father used to gamble and the business went bankrupt. Everything was lost, the bailiffs even took the crockery, and they were left with only what they were wearing. The family went into the workhouse, but my mother went back to her grandmother. A friend found a rented house for them to move into and, as her grandmother was moving, my mother returned once more to her family. This time it was even harder; she said her father would hit her and her mother, and the whole family was very frightened of him.

When she was fourteen Bess decided she couldn't take any more and ran away from home. She met a girl, Maisie, who was in a similar situation. Maisie's mother was a prostitute, and Maisie had also run away from home. The two girls managed to find very badly paid jobs in a laundry and rented a small attic room. They were finding it very hard to live, and one day Maisie went back to ask her mother for help. Bess went into a pub to wait for her, and as she didn't have any money she just sat at a table. A man approached her and sat by her. She was very frightened, but he told her he was a Church Officer, and asked her about her life. She found herself crying, and telling him all about her father. He asked her if she would like to go somewhere where she would be looked after. She later told us that she had been so naïve, and was lucky that he was a genuine Christian. He took her to the home of two sisters, who gave her a meal and a bed. They asked her if she would like to go to the Driffield Church Home and learn to be a Christian. She was terrified her father would find her, and liked the idea of moving away. They took her to Driffield where she was looked after with eight other girls until she was found a place "in service". She went into service as a kitchen maid — the lowest of the low — in a large house. Highfield House was owned by Mr Beans, a Ceylon tea planter. There were twelve staff, and Mam worked there until she was eighteen. She was very happy there, she always said that she felt safe, was well fed, and had her own room, high up in the house, overlooking the wolds. She went back to see the church sisters every week — they were like family to her. She was confirmed, and kept the Bible they gave her all her life. She worked her way up from kitchen maid to under-cook, and each week she would cycle five or six miles with the other girls to go dancing. In 1926, my mother was offered a job as cook at Cranham Nursing Home. She went to see Sister Louise, to ask their advice, and with their approval, she made the move. She learnt that her father had died, and went back to see her mother. Her mother was so happy to see her and told her that after she'd run away, her mother had walked the streets every night looking for her.

Mother met Robert Cruddas, my father, at a dance. Robert was from Bridlington, where he worked as a confectioner at a top restaurant on the seafront during the summer. They often went dancing and saw each other every day until they married. His mother lived in Bridlington with May, one of his sisters. He had another sister, Kathleen, and an adopted brother Reg.

His father, Robert, was one of nine children. The three eldest boys, George, Arthur and Robert, enlisted early in the First World War. Arthur had his own business, a butcher's shop, in Hessle Road, Hull, and gave this up at the beginning of the war so he could enlist. All three were to perish in the conflict. George was killed in July 1916, Arthur in March 1918, and my grandfather Robert was killed by a shell just ten days before the Armistice. I've got a cutting from the local newspaper, with a headline "Bridlington's Roll of Honour" — there's a photo of each of the Cruddas boys, with a eulogy praising them and their family, and stating how proud their country was — what a waste of young lives! Life must have been so difficult for my grandmother, left with four young children to bring up on a very meagre widow's pension.

My mother would never talk about their early married life, but after she died we found some notes my sister Marlene had made of her memories. She had apparently always been worried that I would discover that she had already been pregnant with me before their marriage. In her notes she talks about Robert taking her home to meet her mother. Robert was very thin and thought he was very smart in a large brimmed American hat. When he went to the bathroom, her mother asked her, "What on earth have you brought home?" Bess still wasn't at all close to her mother, but burst into tears and told her she was pregnant. "Well," said her mother, "you'll just have to get married." Mam didn't want to get married, but in those days there wasn't really any other choice. She said later that she knew she didn't love him. In fact, she said, "I didn't really like him, and to tell the truth that was the same for the rest of my life" — how sad! She was six months pregnant when Dad first took her to his home, and very scared. His mother didn't approve either. She was furious. "It's no use crying now, it's a bit late to change your mind now," Annie told her, "you've made your bed, and you'll have to lie on it." The lady Mam worked for at the nursing home bought her a cocktail dress and a cloche hat. They were both twenty-two years old when they were married in Bridlington, and after the ceremony they went back to Robert's mother's house for tea. My parents then went to Goole where my father worked in the winter months.

I can just remember the house Grandma lived in, for I remember staying there as a child. It was a terraced house, with a stream running past the bottom of the garden. The stream was always called by its Yorkshire name "the beck". Dad would tell us tales of how he had tickled trout as a lad. He would lie on the bank, watching the trout swim by, and then gently lower his hand into the water. He would wait for the fish to swim into the shadow of the bank, with the current flowing against them. He said the trout then almost stopped swimming, and he would slowly . . . very slowly . . . bring his curled hand gently into contact with the fish; then with one sharp movement throw the mesmerised trout up onto the bank.

Starting school at the Alexandra Infant and Junior School was a big event in my young life. I've only to close my eyes to remember the oiled floor boards, the big coke stoves and the large fire guards. In winter the stove would be surrounded by crates containing small bottles, each holding a third of a pint of milk. There was a little circle in the top of each cardboard top which pushed out, leaving a hole for inserting a straw. This was fine if it worked, but very often the whole top would push in, and milk squirted everywhere! The milk cost a half-penny a day, but was free if your father was unemployed. The old Victorian school building was similar to many that are still in use today. It had very high rooms, with long, narrow windows. There were gas-lights, which used to give a soft, yellowish light, and purred like a contented cat. I imagine that I must have been about six years old when I went into the junior school. Two memories loom large in my mind of that time — the size and the feel of Mr. Saynor's cane. I can't remember having the cane very often — it was dreaded! It was a short piece of bamboo, about as thick as a thumb, and certainly kept us in order. We had china inkwells and those terrible dip pens. I don't believe that there was ever a worse piece of equipment for a clumsy child. The nib would stutter, causing inkblots everywhere on the page, and I always made a mess. Thank the Lord for pink blotting paper. My best memories are of the stories that Miss Glew read aloud to us. They kept the whole class entranced. I can still recall the atmosphere as she read "The Children of the New Forest" to us. I have this teacher to thank for my life-long love of books. Before I left this school at the age of ten I was already a keen member of the local library, reading three or four books a week.

As my brother and I walked to school we used to pass a large brick building with small unglazed windows near the floor. This was the malt house, which was used for storing barley for the brewing industry. We'd watch the workers laying the grain on the floor, constantly raking it and turning it over. The barley smelled sweet, and we'd stop and sniff the aromatic fumes as we watched the men at work.

The council decided to build a new housing estate in Lime Avenue, and we were able to rent Number 58. It was a small, pleasant estate, which was not yet finished when we moved in. On two sides was the river, with the town and the school, and the railway on the other sides. The ship-building yard, which was adjacent to the town and next to the river, was the largest employer in the area. When I was small, only half the street was finished and the other half was still being built. In those days, when it became dark early the builders used to carry on work by the light of acetylene lamps. This light was produced from acetylene gas made when the granules of carbide were immersed in water. We lads would "obtain" some granules, put them into a lemonade bottle (at the sacrifice of a penny which we could have collected on the empty bottle), added water, replaced the lid — and then threw it very quickly into a ditch full of water. It produced the most satisfactory explosion — almost worth the trouble it caused us with our parents! During the building of the houses, the walls were plastered with sand, lime, horsehair and water. The workmen built pits, the size of an average room, two foot deep, put in the lime and covered it with water. It was then left for a week until it became like thick cream. The men used to place a plank across the pit, so they could stir it with a paddle. Of course, being lads, we just had to cross these planks — and of course I was the lad who inevitably fell in. A burly workman providently rescued me, swilled me down with a hose pipe, tenderly gathered me up in his arms and carried me home. My mother dumped me into a bath — and then what a telling off I received! I hadn't realised what danger I had been in. Although I never repeated this incident, I seemed to find plenty of other dangerous things to do, mostly I think because I tended to act without thinking of the consequences. My best friend was John Moseley, the local policeman's son. We used to take a short cut across the railway crossing, and for sheer devilment would put pennies on the line to see what happened after the train had been over them — yes, like all old timers, I shake my head and complain at the dangerous exploits that today's youngsters get up to! Mam had a new glass bowl light in the main room, and was extremely proud of it. I can see it now, hanging from three chains. I decided to inflate a balloon and, instead of tying a knot, to try putting a marble in the neck to hold the air in. It worked, and I shook it, when there was a large bang and the marble shot upwards, breaking the glass shade — once again I was in trouble! I know my mother was strict, but she was tenderer than my father. I can recall his leather strop which he used to sharpen his razor — and to discipline me! After one particularly severe chastisement, my mother snatched the piece of leather and cut it up so he could never use it on me again.

As I sit here, letting my memory run through the highways and byways of yesteryear, I recall the country lane that ran past the Delph, which was appropriately named Lovers Lane. This lane slowly meandered until it came out in the small village of Hook. We'd walk along this stretch of road on Sunday evenings with Mam and Dad. On summer nights they would stop at the pub, and my brother and I would sit in the garden. I can recall trying to slip out of the pub garden, for on the river bank nearby was the remains of an old barge. It was a great place for exploring — but not, I hasten to add, when in one's best Sunday clothes, and being well-behaved with one's parents. Laurie and I both had bikes. Dad used to buy them second hand from a chap along the street, who made a living from doing up old bikes. In the autumn, for cycling, we wore corduroy lumber jackets. These warm jackets had an elastic band at the bottom and a long zip up the front. I regret to say these were worn less for their warmth than for their usefulness when scrumping apples. A good many apples could be pushed down the front of these jackets. We must have made a comic sight as, with bulging bodies, we beat a retreat chased by an irate farmer with a stick. Like most brothers we often fought with each other. I can remember one occasion when Laurie chased me with the heavy figurine of a cavalier. This was a heavy cast ornament which usually graced Mam's hearth. Thank goodness he didn't catch me and hit me with it — it could have inflicted some damage!

There were two big royal occasions in my childhood. One of these was King George V's Jubilee. We all had the day off school when he visited our little town. I can remember lining up as we all waved our flags and cheered. The second Royal event that I can recall was the coronation of George VI. All the children received a coronation mug, and a bank book from the Yorkshire Bank, with a shilling in it — I wonder whatever happened to that? My father stood for election as a Labour candidate for Goole Borough Council in 1939. I can vividly remember us walking around carrying pole-mounted posters on which "Vote for Cruddas" was printed, and chanting, "Vote, vote, vote for Robert Cruddas". He won by a majority of thirty-one, and was duly welcomed as a Councillor by the Mayor on 12th July. Our boyhood was to be overshadowed by the Second World War. That Autumn there was a sombre mood. The grown-ups seemed worried, there was talk of war, but Laurie and I didn't really understand what was afoot. Just before eleven o'clock on the third of September, Dad called us to sit outside on the bench under the kitchen window and said, "This is a very serious moment in everybody's life. In a few moments the Prime Minister, Mr. Chamberlain, will broadcast to the nation to tell us if war is to be declared." Father sounded very grave, and we duly tried to look as solemn as he obviously expected us to, as we listened to the historic announcement. We didn't know, of course, at the age of seven and ten, how many lives, including our own, would be altered by that declaration.

CHAPTER
TWO

I had by now, progressed to the secondary modern school, and in the first few months failed the equivalent of the "Eleven plus". Everything in that era seems to be blamed on the war, but I really can't blame it for my shortcomings. I just didn't enjoy my time at this school; I found most lessons boring, apart from maths, science and music. The boys left at the elementary schools were never supposed to achieve any scholastic excellence — we were factory fodder. One of the few highlights of my school life was being chosen to play a pirate in *The Pirates of Penzance*. I was rather in love with Mabel and have enjoyed soprano voices ever since. Science seemed to be my forte. I did very well in that subject, and endeavoured to blow myself (and everything else in the neighbourhood) up. Other subjects were less inspiring — horticulture, for example, consisted of the whole class, spread out in a long row across the sports field, methodically weeding it! However, most academic subjects left me cold, I received no encouragement, and all too often I day-dreamed my time away. How often as an adult I have regretted that waste.

By now the war was having a noticeable effect. Rationing had been introduced, everyone in the family had a book of ration tokens, and each person was allowed two ounces of sweets for the week. Strangely enough, I think we ate more sweets from the sweetshop in our family than we had before they were rationed. Father had always brought small chocolate squares home from the bakery kitchens, so money hadn't been spent on sweets. With the advent of rationing we somehow started to buy confectionery. You could blow all this on one chocolate bar or opt for something like boiled sweets which lasted longer; tea, sugar, butter, cheese, meat and eggs were only obtainable on the exchange of coupons. Dried egg was available and housewives became quite adept at using it. Another introduction was tinned Spam; this was made into sandwiches, fritters and many other dishes. Almost everyone grew their own vegetables, and our mothers would preserve them by pickling, salting, drying or bottling. I know that towards the end of the year we got rather tired of green tomato chutney, but Mam made a lovely selection of jams. One of Mam's favourite phrases when anyone complained about the shortages was, "Cheer up, we're short of nowt we've got!" Dad worked for the Co-op Bakehouse at this time, and also had a part-time job as carrier for the Co-op Funeral Service. He was a very keen gardener and had a greenhouse and an allotment where he grew most kinds of vegetables. The rhubarb was so large that Laurie and I could hide amongst the leaves. The carrots were monsters, and I can remember stripping them so we could eat the sweet centres.

In late summer I was often sent out selling Dad's greenhouse tomatoes at four pence a pound. As the war progressed and food rationing became more stringent, we had to make the garden even more productive. We had about twenty rabbits and two ducks. I don't know why we didn't have chickens; perhaps Dad didn't care for them. The rabbits were fed scraps, and as we bred them for food we had to help with the killing. We used to cure the rabbit skins by tacking them onto a piece of plywood, fur side closest to the wood, and then, every few days, I would work handfuls of powdered alum onto the slimy surface. This was done for about a month, then I would take down the skins, knead them to make the pelts supple, and then the skins were ready for Mam to work on. She made them into fur mittens, and I can remember how proud I was when I wore them for the first time! I have always had exceptionally dry skin, and in the winter the skin on my hands would chafe and bleed, so Mam's mittens were a great help in the cold winters. Chicken was a luxury in those days, and particularly so during the war. I can recall having two roast rabbits for one Christmas lunch during the war years. We didn't get bombed in Goole, but I can remember seeing the war planes flying over us. On one occasion we all went rushing from our homes as an RAF plane flew terribly low and then crashed onto the school yard. Thankfully, as it was night-times there were no casualties apart from the crew members.

My mother worked hard, as most women did in those days. Very few people had a vacuum cleaner in our street. Mother used to throw used tealeaves on to the carpet and then brush with a hard broom. At spring-cleaning time I would be sent across the road to hire Mrs. Magilver's little hand vacuum for three pence for the day. On Saturdays Mother used to bake pies and peas to sell. It was quite common to see twenty or thirty folk queuing outside our front door to buy the meat and potato pies. They used to bring their own basins for the "mushy" peas. Father wasn't called up for the forces. As a baker he was in a reserved occupation. He was able, because of his job, to keep us supplied with a great many things that we should otherwise have gone without. To the right of the range in the room — it was always called "the room", we didn't have a dining or sitting room — was a set of tall cupboards which reached from floor to ceiling. Near the top was a shelf on which stood stone jars full of glacé cherries, walnuts, sultanas and currants. If I stood on the second shelf and hung on to the edge of the fourth shelf by one hand, I could just reach these jars. You no doubt know the story of the little monkey and the stone jar; it always makes me remember this episode in my life!

During this period, my uncle Eddie who was in the Royal Navy would spend his leaves with us. He must have been about twenty and was my hero. We never did work out his relationship to us. I know he lived with my parents until he joined the Navy as a boy entrant. He was a champion boxer and swimmer and used to fascinate us with tales of his exploits. I used to help him make his "tittlers". These were hand-rolled cigarettes. He would bring home his allowance of Navy tobacco, spread it out on a sheet of newspaper, shred the loose tobacco and then put a small portion into a little cigarette rolling machine, operating the rollers until the tobacco was neat and compact. The difficult part was taking a cigarette paper, which was gummed down one edge, running the gummed area along one's tongue, then placing it into the machine and rolling it to make a cigarette. I found the operation very difficult to do to his satisfaction at first, but soon got the hang of it, and felt very grown-up helping him. No-one found this strange, cigarette-smoking in those days was quite natural, all adults seemed to smoke. One day Eddie asked if I could swim. "No," I said. "Well, we'll have to do something about that," replied my uncle, "Get yourself some shorts, and I'll take you to the baths." At the swimming baths, Eddie marched me over to the diving board, and told me to follow him up. Once on the top board, he told me to climb on his back, hold on tightly, wrap my legs round his waist, hold my breath and close my eyes! Immediately he dived, and for an exhilarating moment we were flying. I don't remember any fear of the water, or any more swimming lessons, I just swam!

Christmases were quite different then. I am always surprised nowadays to see the amount of presents that children receive, and the quantity of shopping bought in the supermarkets in the run up to Christmas. When I was small, Father didn't get paid until Christmas Eve, and then we went to the market to buy our Christmas fare. The streets were dark and cold, and the market stalls were lit by paraffin-flare lamps. Sitting here writing, I can still imagine myself back there and experience the smells of the paraffin, fruit, spices and meat. Our presents were small, but I am sure that our pleasure on receiving them was just as intense as that experienced by today's youngsters, with their computer games and expensive toys. We had very few shop toys and made a lot of our own entertainment.

There was a gas lamp in the street outside our house. It was a tall, solid piece of street furniture — mind you, it had to be, for as we grew older, we had a rope secured to the cross arm so we could hang on to it and swing round and round.

I'll never forget the fun I had making a puppet theatre, complete with lights, curtains and a trapdoor, from an old cardboard box. I spent hours making the puppet heads. I started off with a lump of Plasticine and made a model head, complete with the crucial neck and exaggerated facial features. I then made flour and water paste. As this was made with boiling water, I wasn't allowed to do it myself — and I can remember pestering my poor mother until she found time to do it for me. While the paste was being made, I tore pieces of old newspaper into stamp-sized pieces. These pieces were pasted thickly over the model head, and when dried I had perfect papier-mâché models. Now, all I had to do was to badger Mam into making the clothes for my puppets to disguise my hand movements. I can remember the pleasure I had from this achievement, and the hours of entertainment we had with these puppets.

However, my mother certainly didn't appreciate my pet mice; I know I thought she was very strange! I had black, chocolate-coloured and white mice, and they were very friendly. I would sometimes bring them into the house, where I would build a maze from children's bricks, covering them with a pane of glass. I used to have great fun with these until one day they escaped. Mother was so cross, and no more mice were allowed into the house! Another of my experiments was very time-consuming. I tried to make a gadget which would write automatically! I made a series of wooden channels, with a paddle at one end, and a sort of pen at the other. I then filled the channels with water, and when I plunged the paddles at varying speeds, the resulting wave would make the pen work — a sort of rudimentary Morse code!

Laurie and I always had a trolley, which we made from an old apple box and four wheels. The back half of the trolley was formed from the box, so you could sit on it, with your feet on the front cross member to steer it. We had various additions to make life more exciting, such as a cover over the box to make a covered wagon, and various levers to act as brakes, etc. Dad's rabbits always needed hay and in the summer (why is it that there always seemed to be such long, hot summers in those days?) it was our job to fetch the hay. Laurie and I would take the trolley to a field at the back of the cemetery, about two miles away. Then came the fun of playing in the hay before we collected it, piling it high on the trolley, and then pushing it home.

A stray cat was a regular visitor to our garden, and we'd feed him, but he was always a bit wary of us. One day he turned up looking very ill, and I was told to take him to the vet. I tucked him into my jacket, and walked to the veterinary clinic by the docks. The vet eyed me warily — "Have you brought your shilling?" he asked. I wordlessly offered it to him; he took the cat, wrapped it in a large towel, and then took a none too clean looking penknife from his pocket. "See, laddie," and he showed me the cat's ear, "This fellow's got an abscess, and I'll have to lance it." He immediately cut into the swelling and gunge shot everywhere. He handed the cat back and showed me out — all over in minutes!

We also befriended a stray mongrel dog, Prince. He was such a friendly dog, but he had a bad habit of running off, not just anywhere, but always to the river where the banks down to the water were soft, squelchy mud, at least six inches deep. After Prince had shown us several times just how muddy he could get, Mother put her foot down and he was shown the door.

After Prince came Peggy, a well-behaved springer spaniel. We would take her with us to the "ditch". The ditch was a stretch of water, about four feet wide, which divided the railway embankment from the fields. Laurie and I would meet our friends to play there. We walked the edges of the fields, picking and eating peas — I've never since tasted peas so sweet and tasty. The ditch led to an area of patchy grass where we had target practice with our catapults, firing ball-bearings or stones. We would also make swords from the reeds, and spent many happy hours perfecting our sword practice! Bull-rushes also made fantastic weapons. We would pick these and hit each other with them. It was very satisfying when the ripe pods exploded, covering us with a shower of seeds! If we could find any kindling, we would light a fire. Sometimes we managed to forage potatoes from the fields and bake them in the fire. How good they tasted, despite the black patches and the ash. If we were lucky enough to get hold of a packet of Symingtons soup, we would mix this up with some potatoes, peas and water, and heat it up in an old Ostermilk can — what a banquet this was! Often we'd take a rope with us and tie it to a tree which overhung the river. Then we would swing out on it over the water, playing at being Tarzan. Every so often one of us young dare-devils would fall in, and then have to attempt to dry out over the bonfire. We were never quite sure which was the lesser of the two evils — to go home guilty and soaking wet, or relatively dry and smelling of wood smoke. Our Mam had a habit of catching hold of our ears when we returned home and, drawing us close to her, would smell our hair, to see if we had been playing with fire. All too often the telltale smoke lingered, and then woe betide us!

Another favourite place for us to explore was Goole Docks. Many different types of boats came into the docks. Before the war we used to watch the large white Danish butter boats discharging their cargo. There were also large silos where grain was stored. One Christmas I was very excited to receive a cardboard model of one of these silos, which I had to assemble. It came complete with a little sack of grain, and I can remember having great fun with it. There was a very large warehouse which stored monkey nuts. Laurie and I somehow got in, and escaped with our useful jackets stuffed full of nuts! We loved to play at the docks; there were so many exciting nooks and crannies, which just begged to be investigated. There were usually very small cob boats tied up, which we would "liberate" and I learned to scull across the water, steering with the one oar at the back of the boat. When I was about eleven I discovered how to make quite satisfactory fireworks. There was a brick air-raid shelter by the back door which I used for my secret operations. The fireworks were made from a mixture of saltpetre, sulphur and charcoal. I would make a "banger" using a cardboard tube and a piece of saltpetre-soaked paper for a fuse. This was taken to the Delph and placed inside an oil drum, then I would light the fuse and retire sharply. You can imagine the very satisfactory explosion! Another experiment was to take a thimbleful of potassium permanganate, add one drop of glycerine into the centre and stand back. This would self-combust without any further intervention on my part — a very gratifying happening.

On one of our trips to the river bank, Laurie and I came across a contractors' hut which was open. We explored the inside and found a strange-looking machine, about the same height as Laurie, with a handle sticking out of the side. It was an open invitation — handles were surely made for turning, weren't they? We cranked the handle several times, with no result . . . boring. We decided to try once more, and suddenly there was a tremendous bang, a huge puff of smoke, and the whole machine leapt upward to hit the roof of the shed! My brother and I scrambled to get out of the door, and ran off as quickly as possible. I now realise that we had been playing with a petrol-operated road tamper, and had been lucky to escape without injury.

As you can see, we really didn't need television, video and expensive games to amuse us — we were well able to amuse ourselves. The children of today appear to have so much, but in so many ways they are wrapped in cotton wool — it's difficult for them to find the freedom and adventure that we all enjoyed. The only amusement which was ready made for us was the Saturday cinema. It cost tuppence to get in to see Flash Gordon and the Clay Men, Laurel and Hardy and Tarzan — what value for tuppence. The pictures in those days were continuous, so if you went in half way through the film it was of no great consequence, you just sat there until you saw the whole film! Laurie can remember coming to the pictures with me and my friends, and staying on, after we left, to watch the film through again. There was a great panic at home as Mother didn't know where he was, and Dad had to go to the cinema and have him brought out. Alas, these carefree days were to come to a sudden end when I became fourteen. Childish things had to be put away, school finished with, as the hard cruel world of work beckoned.

CHAPTER
THREE

I was fourteen on the sixteenth of January 1943, and the time had come to leave school and venture forth into the big wide world — and what a shock this big wide world turned out to be. I was to be an apprentice electrician at the shipyard, but to my dismay I couldn't start for three months. In the meantime, arrangements had been made for me to have a temporary job. I was to work at Brough Aircraft Factory near Hull where the Skua bombers were made for the Fleet Air Arm. The factory started work at eight o'clock, and I had a good hour's travelling time. It was a great shock to my system to have to rise at six, walk a good way to the station and catch the seven o'clock train. I will never forget my first morning. It was cold and foggy as I stood on the platform, clutching my sandwiches and gas mask. The train pulled in, competing against the fog, just as if it were a fog-making machine. There appeared to be hundreds of men and women attempting to board this dirty, belching monster. All the men seemed to have a cap or trilby pulled firmly on to their heads and the women all had scarves tied around their heads, as if in some vain effort to keep the fog at bay. The carriages were very basic, with no corridor, and each compartment seated twelve. I pushed my way into a carriage, the door slammed, and there was a shrill blast from the guard's whistle. There was a final banging of doors along the length of the train, a judder backwards and forwards and then, with a leap and a clanging of metal on metal, we were off. The inside windows were wet with condensation, and most people were smoking. The smoke from the engine clung tenaciously to the outside windows and the smoke inside clung to the condensation. The heat from our bodies made even more condensation, and I was very warm and smoky when we arrived at our destination.

Several hundred people got off the train, all with gas masks and shoulder bags containing necessities such as their sandwiches and the *Daily Herald*. The men and women appeared to form into two queues which went through two tunnel-like buildings from whence emanated a regular ding-ding sound. I was soon to find out that this was the sound of the time-keeping clock, and was made when you put your works card into its mouth and pressed a lever, so causing the bell to ring and the time to print onto the card. If you were up to a quarter of an hour late, money was docked from your pay, but heaven help you if you were later than that, for you were then locked out and lost a day's pay.

I had been told to report to the gatehouse. A young lad, Alf, not much older than myself but very confident, was waiting to take me to the foreman in the Parts shop. Alf appeared to be a chirpy, cocky lad who seemed to know his way about, and I followed him rather sheepishly. We threaded our way through what seemed to be thousands of people, all intent on getting to their own place in the factory. The sheer size astonished me; the building seemed big enough to play two football games, and still have room to spare. There were perhaps a dozen aircraft in various stages of being built. I had never been anywhere near an aircraft before, so you can imagine my shock as we made our way across the main assembly bay. There was such a hubbub of noise, the scream of the compressed air drills, the people shouting to one another, the clamour of machinery, a cacophony of strange sounds. I tried to absorb all the sights and sounds, which were interspersed with comments from my guide. What a day — I thought I would never find my way about, but I was proud to think that I had actually been allowed into the place.

The jobs I was allowed to do were very basic. I can remember making special washers from aluminium. I was in trouble with the foreman on one occasion (at least!) for I was making a model Spitfire aeroplane out of a copper penny. I had put this on the grinding machine and had not known, until bawled out by a horrified foreman, that you were not supposed to put soft metals on a grinding machine. When you are fourteen you do a lot of fetching and carrying, and having your leg pulled. "Go and fetch me a long stand from Joe Bloggs," I was told. I duly requested the item from Bloggs, and was left waiting. I fidgeted and nervously coughed, but everyone ignored me. Eventually I was asked, "Well, lad, was that 'stand' long enough for you?" On another occasion I was asked to fetch some yellow sparks for the grinder, and spent some time wandering about trying to find them! The trouble was that after such happenings one became wary of any requests. When asked to get some aluminium normalised, I looked incredulous and had to be convinced that all aluminium had to be normalised, which was a form of annealing. There was one strange outcome to this short career. I had a young cousin, Colin, who was about eight years old at this time. I rather think I impressed him with my tales of the aircraft, and I can remember making him a toy aeroplane. Our families lost touch, and when we met up, both in our sixties, I found to my surprise that Colin had made a very successful career in aviation, and has recently written and had published quite a few books on the subject. In the summer of 1994, my wife and I spent a weekend with Colin and his wife Thelma in their beautiful thatched, chocolate-box cottage near Shaftsbury, and we were able to catch up on ancient family history.

As my three months' period came to a close, I was pleased, for this wasn't the job for me. I'd found it interesting but it was just an in-fill period and there was no depth to the training. I found myself anxiously waiting to take up my apprenticeship in the shipyard. The apprenticeship was at Crag's Shipyard on the River Ouse. Although the shipyard was new to me, it wasn't to my family. My mother had worked for several years at Crag's shipyard. She used to cycle to work each morning for eight o'clock. She operated a lathe, turning parts that weighed nearly a hundredweight. She had to struggle to lift these on her own. I can remember being so surprised to see my little mother managing to cope with these monsters. It was incredible what women did during the war years. Now it was my turn to cycle to the shipyard. This first morning I had to report to Mr Shuttleworth, the head of the electrical company, who was going to pay me seven shillings and sixpence a week as an apprentice electrician.

Up to this period, the traditional method of constructing ships was generally to construct a network of steel beams and angles, and then clad this frame with plates of steel by riveting. The ship looked like the skeleton of some monster fish, supported by enormous baulks of timber, and this in turn was enveloped in a tracery of scaffolding. Each plate was lifted into its place by one of the many lifting cranes. A straightforward plate would have been pre-drilled, as would the rib of steel it was to be fixed to. It was first bolted, and the crane dispensed with, and then it was the riveters' turn. A team consisted of three men. The first was the heater. As his name implies, he heated the rivets up to a bright red in a small foot-powered furnace, then he threw the rivet to the second man in the team, who caught it in a tin tray, picked it up with tongs and poked it into the holes that lined up in the rib and plate. He then held a weight on the head of the rivet, which gave a firm hold for the third member of the team to use his pneumatic hammer on the still-hot end of the rivet, making a very good joint. A riveting hammer must be one of the noisiest tools in the world as it beats against the rivet. The whole of the structure reverberated. Just imagine — there could have been fifty riveters playing this tune!

As I joined the shipyard a big change was happening in the industry, inasmuch that the ships were now being pre-fabricated. The ships (a small one could have been about ten thousand tons) were designed so that different sections could be made in various parts of the country. These were then transported to the shipyard and assembled, mainly by electrical welding, to make the complete hull of the ship. The pre-fabricated parts, each one weighing up to one hundred tons or more, were of assorted shapes and sizes, and made up a three-dimensional jigsaw, finally emerging as the finished ship. The parts were manipulated by huge cranes, towering above the site. These cranes were known as Goliaths, the very name itself giving some idea of their size. Most ships were built on the slipway until the hull and bridge works were completed, then launched into the river and taken into dock for the fitting-out. Fitting-out was the process of installing all the equipment to permit the ship to carry out its intended task.

I found the launching of a ship so impressive. A ship was started by laying the base (the keel) on a special sloping runway, made up of a series of very solid cradles. As the ship grew, so did these cradles, extending to suit the curve of the hull. At the launch, steel ropes and chains restrained the whole from sliding into the river. Selected ones were released, whilst others were anchored to piles of chain that were dragged along the ground to steady the movement down the slope into the river. As the ship struck the water — a good job partly done — everyone cheered and waved. There still remained the fitting-out to be done by an army of various tradesmen, and this is where I fitted in. There would have been about a dozen electricians, and four or five apprentices. The electrics were installed in lead-covered wire which was laid in neat multiple rows, secured with brass clips. After installation these were lovingly polished, a great deal of work, bearing in mind that this was war-time. We used to install de-gauzing equipment — this was effectively a coil of wire round the ship which de-magnetised it, and prevented the explosion of magnetic mines.

I was enjoying my work, and had expected to complete my apprenticeship at the shipyard, but it was not to be. My father had to move to Tipton in the West Midlands under the Essential Works Order. Away from wife and family the inevitable happened, and he met another woman. He was lodging at a public house and his landlady wrote to Mother, warning her that if she wanted to save her marriage she should lose no time in joining him. She sold the furniture, packed up our belongings and in December 1943, we followed him. We all found it a great shock as we travelled into the Midlands by train. We gazed around, finding it impossible to see where one town finished and the next started. It was so dreary after our home town, and we all became very quiet and depressed. We'd been living in a modern house in Yorkshire, with a beautiful garden and a greenhouse, but accommodation in Tipton was hard to come by. Dad had tried to find us a decent home, but we found ourselves living in a small house, one up, one down with an attic and cellar, and a toilet and tap outside in a communal yard. Father decorated it, installed a gas cooker at the head of the stairs which led to the cellar, and made a workshop in the attic. The one bedroom was fairly large and he divided this into two, one part for my parents, the other for Laurie and me. Laurie and I hated it, and Mam was very bitter, but there was nowhere else for us to live. She never really settled down happily here, and always regretted the loss of her home and friends, although she spent the rest of her life in the Midlands. Laurie was still at school, and I had to look for another apprenticeship. Fortunately jobs were quite easy to come by as there were so many men in the forces, and I soon found a job at Harris Electrical Contractors.

By the start of 1944 I was going to night school three nights a week. In my spare time I enjoyed going to the pictures, and this is where I was heading one night when I arrived at the bus stop and saw a very attractive young lady. I was quite a shy young man, but, not possessing a watch, I plucked up enough courage to ask her for the time. We sat next to each other on the bus and again in the cinema, so once again plucking up my nerve, I asked if I could walk her home. It was a beautiful moonlit night, and we had a pleasant walk, with rather stilted conversation as we were both rather timid. That was my first meeting with Jean Reynolds, who was to become my wife. She was tiny, standing at only four foot ten, and very gentle. She was inclined to be plump, with brown eyes, and light brown hair. Our courting consisted mainly of walks along the canal, and going to the pictures at the weekend. We'd sometimes book a double seat at the Alhambra Cinema, Dudley Port, or walk the three miles to Coseley to see the film at the Clifton; then it was a long walk home, a chaste kiss or two, and I would walk back dreamily to Tipton. I didn't own an overcoat, and would borrow my father's heavy tweed coat! We'd sometime get the bus to Sutton Park at Sutton Coldfield, or visit May, her married sister. Sometimes Jean would come to my house for the weekend, where she would spend the night on the sofa, whilst I slept in the attic with Bill — no hanky panky in those days! We fell in love very quickly and neither of us ever had eyes for anyone else.

Jean lived with her family in Tipton, in a small house which also came out onto a courtyard. In the courtyard there was the brew house, where the washing was done, and the outside toilet which was used by all the houses — about six of them — around this little area. The house itself was two up and two down — that's two rooms downstairs and two upstairs — and none of the rooms was more than ten feet square. There was gas lighting, and the stairs led out of the kitchen, which reduced it still further in size. There was a cast iron fireplace with an oven on one side, a table and a small settee under the window. There was a gas ring on the window-sill above the settee, and Jean's young sister Rita was seriously burned when a kettle of water which was boiling on the ring tipped over on to her. She was very ill and died as a result of her injuries. It's difficult to imagine such living conditions nowadays, but in those days living accommodation was difficult to come by for the working class. Their house was extremely tiny for the family. As well as the parents, there was Jean, her twin brother Dick, and her older sisters Olive and May. I can remember Jean telling me that her mother would take them out for the day to Baggeridge, which is a very, very long walk, at least five miles each way. They had to go through Sedgley, which is quite steep, with the children taking turns in pushing the pram. Those rare days out were the only holidays Jean and the family enjoyed. There was never any money for proper holidays.

It was about this time that World War Two ended. Victory in Europe — VE day — was celebrated on the 8th May 1945, and the celebrations were great. We went to a bonfire party at the pub where my father had lodged — I think there were quite a few sore heads that night! I had to find a new apprenticeship, as I was determined to become an electrician. One of my first jobs was working at Wrights Forge in Tipton. I'd been told to report to the chief electrician, Doug Perks. He was a large, pleasant character, but I soon learned that when he said "jump", one jumped. He told me that my first job every morning would be to get a fire going in the old iron stove. "Look," he told me; "This is the way to do it." He had in his hand a "squirty" oil can, which I found was filled with paraffin. He started to squirt this into a hole at the base of the stove, pumping away until the place seemed to be full of acrid mist, then there was a gigantic "pooph", the stove was alight with a vengeance and one could see the flames through a crack in the chimney. Then followed a gentle roar as the chimney started to glow. "Now," he instructed me, "Shovel some coke into that top aperture, and get the kettle on." I did as instructed, found a huge old kettle, and was then handed an iron frying pan, and shown how to make breakfast! This became my routine each morning, and then I was set to work in the electrical maintenance department. The test house fascinated me for it was here that they stretched samples of metal until they broke with a loud 'bang.' This was the part of the forge which made gigantic shafts for ships engines and the like

As a result of the peace my father changed jobs from armoured car manufacturing to his normal trade of baker and confectioner. This also brought us to another house, at 259b Castle Street in Dudley. It was a beautiful old house at the back of Castle Street, belonging to Woodhouse, the bakers. It had a large copper fireplace framed by mahogany, with shutters on the windows, and was three storeys high — luxury for us. Dudley has now been re-developed and our old house has been knocked down. I now find it difficult to visualise where it stood. Dad was still very interested in politics; he joined the local Labour Club, and was very proud of his association with George Wigg, the Labour politician.

My first job working for Harris Electrical was at the Thomas Dudley foundry on the Birmingham New Road. At this time no plastic was used in sanitary ware, and Thomas Dudley used to manufacture cast iron lavatory tanks. The floor inside the foundry was several inches deep in black sand; at one end was a tall cupola about fifty foot high, with an open mouth at the top. A mixture of old scrap iron, coke and pig iron would be fed into the mouth, and then the molten metal would exit into a fireclay trough a few feet from the floor. This molten liquid was then dispensed by hand-ladles into the various moulds. As the metal was poured from the ladles, sparks, smoke, dust and smells rose into the air, making a fog that caused one to cough and eyes to water. The electricians had to work in the roof supports, which were all L-shaped angled iron, but due to the conditions, there was always a pyramid of dirt on top of them and installing cables along these was dangerous and dirty work — no health and safety concerns in those days!

The finishing department was another hive of activity, with men working on immense double-ended grinding machines, taking off the rough parts of the moulding. These were then taken to Nellie, a voluptuous lady who was the painter. The painting was done by sliding the cast down a large drainer into a huge tank of thin red paint, then out the other side to drain. Nellie was dressed for the part with an apron, then several layers of hessian sacking. I can see her now, her bare arms immersed in the tank of paint, with cheeks as red as her arms, and a lovely wide smile. Another of my jobs was to convert the old gas installations in houses to electricity. I must have been very slim in those days, as I had to get under the floorboards. The space was about sixteen inches by eight inches, the width between the joists and a couple of floorboards! As a young electrician I decided to moonlight and to do some jobs on my own, and I was quite successful. I was putting sockets in houses, at two pounds fifty shillings each, to make myself a bit of extra money. There was a shop in the town, the Fifty Shilling Tailors, who wanted me to put some new lights in. Fluorescent fittings were just coming out, and this is what they wanted. However, a great deal of Dudley Town was still DC, and fluorescent lights won't work properly on DC. They used to go black on one end, so one had to put in a switch to turn the polarity round, to make it go black on the other end! I put them in, and they were the first fluorescent lights in Dudley. My younger brother Laurie helped me; he was very much a youngster compared with me in those days, for he was two and a half years younger than me and still at school. We called ourselves Jackson Electrical. Jackson was our mother's maiden name — we thought it was better not to use our own name!

Conscription was still in force in 1947. All young men over the age of eighteen had to go into the forces for two years. On the 16th January I received my conscription papers and went for my medical. I had really wanted to go into the Navy, like Uncle Eddie, or the Air Force, but I had flat feet and they didn't want me! I had to go into the Army instead. The day I had to join my unit we had snow, snow and yet more snow. It was a Thursday (one always joined your unit on a Thursday — like polling day) and there was little transport, and one would certainly never have dreamed of not going. Jean came with me on the bus to

Wednesbury, then she got a bus back to Tipton, and I had to carry on to Lichfield — walking and getting lifts as I could. One lift was on the back of a tractor. There wasn't much traffic braving the weather. I can't imagine today's pampered teenagers making that sort of journey. They are used to being ferried around by car from their earliest days, and I'm sure would refuse to walk in such conditions, and perhaps rightly so, their parents wouldn't allow it. I finally got to the barracks late that day, tired and cold after walking most of the way — but I was going to be in the Army — and that's another story!

CHAPTER
FOUR

I eventually arrived, with several other nervous looking young men, at the Victorian mausoleum that was Whittington Barracks. This was a series of oblong three-storey buildings around a big square. At the entry was a soldier on guard. "New recruits?" he enquired. "Yes," we replied and he directed us through the snow to the mess hall, where we were given a very welcome mug of tea. There were a couple of hundred new recruits by then. We were told that we would be at the Wellington Barracks for six weeks, and during this basic training we would learn the facts about the army, what and who to salute, the ranking system, where we could and couldn't go — and we weren't going to be allowed out of camp during these six weeks. There would be a competition between the various groups to see which would be the best group at the end of the six weeks, and then we might be able to go home for a week-end — a bit of an incentive! We were all put into platoons, A, B or C, divided into groups of twenty-eight, and given directions to our billets. The billet had twenty-eight beds and lockers. Our first job was to fill in paperwork, and then we were each given our eight-figure identification number. That number would be our "name" throughout our army career. My number was 19141805.

We were then sent to be "kitted-out" — or issued with the clothes which would change us from a civilian into a soldier. I was given two sets of itchy underwear, and had to bear in mind that there was no Mam to do my washing and look after my clothes now, so one had to be a bit careful. There were khaki denim trousers and jacket, with pockets for putting maps and essentials in, and there would be a dress uniform, but we weren't going to get our best uniform until they saw how we shaped up to a rough six weeks' training. We also got a pair of boots. I wasn't used to boots, most people weren't, but boots we had to wear. There were also gaiters, which went round the bottom of our trousers to tidy them up. We also got a khaki webbing belt with brass bits on which had to be kept polished. There was also an ammunition pouch which clipped on — we didn't know anything about ammunition yet, but we'd learn! Finally we were each given a tin helmet and a forage cap, and a big white kit-bag, and were sent back to our billets to find a bed and locker. Each bed in the billet had three "biscuits" on — what were biscuits? A biscuit was a square mattress, about a third of the size of a single bed, and these three biscuits made up the mattress for the bed. No sheets, just three prickly grey blankets and a round hard pillow like a sandbag! We started chatting, finding out about each other. Most of my room-mates were from the Stoke area. I could have felt a bit strange as a Yorkshire man, but I get on with most people, and we soon got used to each other.

We were all feeling a bit hungry by then, and found that there was a NAAFI, a canteen where you paid for food, so we made our way there. I think the next thing I remember is six o'clock the next morning, when a corporal marched up and down the room, shouting, "Get out of bed, get out! Get washed and shaved, then form two ranks outside, and you'll get some breakfast. After breakfast you're going to learn how to march!" This business about learning how to march took up a lot of our time for the next six weeks! From slow marching to quick marching, to about turn, right turn, left turn — it's surprising how many people didn't know their left from their right! Another bit of kit we were issued with was the shorts, singlet and plimsolls for cross-country running. We used to do about five miles fairly regularly. This wasn't too bad in gym kit, but we found later that we had to do this in full kit, and were practically on our knees by the time we returned to barracks. We also learnt how to carry a rifle with us — and they were heavy! It was certainly an experience, teaching discipline and blind obedience, and at the end of six weeks we knew how to march, stand to attention and pay attention, and dress smartly. I missed my home and Jean, of course, but we wrote each other long and loving letters.

At the end of the six weeks, it was decided that with what they had learned about me, they were going to send me to the Royal Engineers. I had to go for three months to the School of Electrical and Mechanical Engineers at Chatham in Kent, to learn some basic engineering skills. At that stage I didn't know how to use a lathe or various other machines. I really liked Chatham. It was a large school and I learnt a lot of skills, including roller skating! I had to learn how to mend lead-covered cables which went under ground. One had to actually plumb the lead with a blowlamp and solder. Using leg spikes, we had to climb up poles, thirty or forty foot, to repair wires at the top. At this stage, I was doing lots of things I'd never done before, and it was great. At the end of the course we had engineering tests. One test was to cut a hole exactly one inch square in a piece of quarter plate, and then make a piece of one inch steel to fit in the hole so exactly that you couldn't tell there were two pieces there. I used to have fairly regular forty-eight hour passes from Chatham, which meant I could go home to Dudley. I used to go by train. Coming back I would catch the train from Snow Hill, Birmingham, to London and then catch the milk train at four o'clock in the morning back to Chatham.

On finishing at Chatham, they decided to send me to Farnborough to learn the heavy engineering side. This was to include building Bailey bridges. These are bridges constructed over a river using manpower, without any mechanical lifting aids. You assemble it on one side of the river, and then roll it over until it touches the other side. It's heavy work, but it does the job. A couple of years ago we went out for dinner with some of Lorna's friends. After the meal Tony and I started chatting, and found that we had both been doing the same training, in the same place, just six months apart. Lorna and Pat looked up from their brandies with astonishment, as we glided across the floor our arms in front of us, fists clenched. Of course they *quite* understood when we explained that we had been trying to remember how we carried a panel for the Bailey bridge!

After learning about Bailey bridges, we moved on to making bridges out of timber and rope. This was quite fascinating, the sort of thing I really enjoyed. Another part of our training was how to find mines and take them out, crawling along on your tummy, prodding the sand with a bayonet to see if you could feel a mine! We had to learn all the various types of explosives in case you came across them in your army career. There was one explosive device called a "beehive". This was a small container about a foot diameter, which we used to tie onto a column under a bridge or the like and put the fuse in. The fuse was a long piece of rope-like material. When you light one end, the flame slowly travels to the other end. One would get out of the way — and a few minutes later "BANG!" It effectively drilled a hole in the brick column a couple of inches diameter and eight inches deep, and we would use this hole to fill with other explosives so one could blow the whole lot up. I certainly enjoyed this part of my training; it was like being a schoolboy again!

There was now talk of us being sent abroad, and I found I'd been booked on a ship from Liverpool, going to Malta. My mother was having another child at the age of forty-two, she wasn't very well, and I tried hard to get compassionate leave to visit her. However, the Army wasn't having that, and I wasn't to see my new baby sister Marlene for some time. The boat we travelled on was the Cunard White Star S.S *Scythia*. It was a terrible journey, everyone, and I do mean everyone, was seasick going through the Bay of Biscay. There were a few thousand people on this boat, the toilets had little ledges around the doors, and the floors were full of vomit — it was revolting, to say the least. We passed Cape Finisterre and saw the fishermen fishing for sardines. Once I found my sea-legs I wasn't too bad, but some people were sick the whole time. Eventually we arrived at Valletta, Malta, but it wasn't a very pleasant journey. Jean wrote to me with the request "Please don't find another girl over there". I was such a naïf young man, quite cautious around women, so it wasn't very likely!

Malta was warm and very exciting for a young man who'd never been abroad before. We knew that we should be there for three weeks, but we didn't know where our eventual posting would be. We were told, "Whatever you do, don't go wandering down the Gut." Malta's famous "Strait Street", known affectionately to all as the "GUT", housed Malta's infamous red light district. This amazing narrow street, stretching as it did from one end of Valletta to the other, was alive every night with the sounds of endless parties emanating from small bars and nightclubs and was where the ladies of ill repute plied their trade. Of course, we thought "Why not?" It was like a red rag to a bull telling us not to go. So a great many inexperienced 18-year olds went straight to the red light district to gawp. The "ladies" called out, "Hello, Johnny, come over here, I'll make you happy Johnny!" but we turned tail and ran!

Soon we found out that we were to be sent to Tobruk on the north coast of Libya. That was another hellish journey, about thirty of us squaddies in what was no more than a large barge. We were bolted below deck; we couldn't even get on to deck to look. We were all pleased to reach Tobruk, where we had a short rest before moving on, and I shall always be grateful to the members of the Salvation Army who welcomed us with cups of tea. Tobruk was a name to be conjured with for during the war the Germans had besieged the place, and no-one could get in or out. It was now just a big British Army camp.

Our barracks were in the Cyrenaica district; Cyrene was an old Roman town on the north coast of Libya. The Greeks founded the city of Cyrene, and then in 74 B.C it was taken over by the Romans. They joined Cyrenaica to Rome as a Roman Province, and Cyrene became one of the greatest intellectual and artistic centres of the world — now it was a British army base! The Roman buildings remaining were incredible. It was near the sea, and there was a wonderful swimming pool which had been built by the Romans. This was surrounded by columns and lined with mosaics. The sea ran into the pool, and effectively the water was changed with every change of tide. It was such a beautiful place.

We were taken to our billet which was to be our home for the next twelve months or so. The camp was made up of tents, and it was fantastic to have a decent meal, for they fed us as soon as we got there. We were then given our instructions and told that we were going to be supervising German prisoners of war. They were still in camps and were re-building Benghazi, which had been bombed during the war. The war had ended in 1945, but the prisoners were working before their repatriation and my job was to supervise them — looking back, whether I had sufficient experience for this responsibility was very debatable! During the next month or two I was given a motor-bike for transport. I used to drive over to Benghazi either in a five-ton Bedford truck with a group of other people, or would ride on my motor-bike. By then we were all in our tropical uniform, khaki shirt and shorts, socks and boots, and I used to burn my legs when I rode my bike as the metal was so hot!

I found I was supervising the replacement of lots of windows. Part of the job was instructing local Arabs how to cut glass with a diamond glass-cutter, but first of all I had to learn myself! These sheets of glass were eight foot by four foot. For the first month I was showing people how to handle these things, how to cut them so that they would fit the windows. There were various other jobs I had to do, even instructing the locals who were being employed by the Army how to clean a cess pit out. Some of the Germans were doing the carpentry work and I had a young Arab assistant, Omi — my "gofer" who fetched and carried for me and taught me a little Arabic. I can still recall "Please" — min fadhlik and "Thank you" — shukran.

There had been a large harbour at Benghazi, but all that remained now were sunken boats sticking up at very strange angles out of the water. It was hot and sunny, very pleasant after England's snow. I used to go back to the camp at Cyrenaica to eat in the mess tent. We slept six to a tent. I managed to make myself a little crystal set so that I could listen to the news. At one time I also had a pet chameleon; he would sit on the ropes inside the tent, walking backwards and forwards, and we used to feed him with tit bits. We had reasonable meals and we always had water melon for dessert. The cooks would cut up large melons into pieces for us to help ourselves. My wife finds it very funny that the most exotic food I tried in Libya was egg and chips which we bought in the souk! I never did get to have a swim in that marvellous pool, but I remember that there was an image of these broken columns on my shoulder flash to indicate that we were with the Cyrenaica force. The columns were white on a dark background, and the flash was very smart.

We had trips into the mountains occasionally on Army wagons, but apart from that we didn't move very far from Benghazi or our base. We were given free issue of fifty cigarettes each week — no wonder so many people smoked! Most of the prisoners made things in their spare time using aluminium from the crashed aircraft lying around the place. I was given a present of a cigarette lighter with "Benghazi 1948" engraved on it. Unfortunately this was stolen on the boat coming back to England. My time in Libya came to an end in May 1949. The journey back wasn't bad at all, not like the journey out there. My demobilization papers came through, and though we were strongly encouraged to remain in the army, I was keen to get my life back. I've just found my army papers and they state, "Has done well in his trade — hard working, polite, sober, honest — character very good!" We were given demob suits, and soon I was on my way back to Dudley, and to Jean who had waited for me. It was great to get back. The two years had gone by quite quickly, though, and it was an experience I wouldn't have missed for the world, it taught me such a lot. I had learnt how to get on with people from different backgrounds and cultures, learned a little Arabic and German, how to receive and give orders, to take responsibility and to look after myself. This was a marvellous experience and a good basis for future life, and I sometimes think that some form of conscription would give many of our present day youngsters much needed self-discipline.

CHAPTER
FIVE

It felt strange to be back in England, and especially strange to come home to a little sister. The army now behind me, I had to find a job again. I was taken on by Postings Electrical Contractors, in conjunction with Graham Hill and Poole, mining engineers. Because my employers had diverse interests, I was doing a lot of different jobs, and one interesting one was at the Wrens Nest in Dudley. The Wrens Nest is a very ancient area of land full of caverns where they extracted lime in the 18th and 19th centuries. These caverns, some as big as a great church inside, were beginning to erode. There were slips from the roof and the authorities were worried about the danger this would cause, so the council wanted to have a warning system to alert them when there were rock falls. It was decided that the cathedral-like cavern would have wires criss-crossed from one side to the other so that any falling rocks would set off an electrical alarm on the surface. To get to this cavern we had to go to the entrance, which was called the Severn Sisters, through a series of caves, down winding paths through the caverns — there were no maps; one had to find one's own way. At the bottom was a canal about ten feet wide which went right through the Wrens Nest. There was a fallen tree stretched across the canal from one side and across the water to the other side, and we could get across this by balancing precariously. It was a bit difficult, but the makeshift bridge did the job. We then reached the large cavern where we were to work.

There were two of us, the electrician and myself. It was very dark in there, so working conditions were difficult. There was an airshaft up to the surface, which was about one hundred and fifty foot high. It gave a small glimmer of light — but not very much. We had a young apprentice who was a disaster. When he was asked to make a billy-can of tea by the electrician, he put a whole packet of tea in! One day we needed some porcelain connectors to use in the cavern, and he was sent to the wholesalers to collect a box. We were hard at work in the cavern when we heard him shout down the airshaft, "Watch out, I'm sending the connectors down." Before we could warn him, he'd thrown the box down. The box containing a gross of porcelain connectors broke, and the whole lot shattered all over the floor — that apprentice didn't last long! We fixed all the wires, zigzagged under the arched, rocky roof of the cavern, so that if any of the wires were broken by a rock fall, various lights would come on at a board on the surface — that was a different job, to say the least.

My title altered to "Improver", and I could now be sent out on jobs by myself. You soon grew up in those days; the very nature of work dictated that. For instance, one of my jobs was in a clay pit, the Hadcroft Colliery, which was about one hundred and fifty feet deep. We would be taken down to the working area by means of a cage, which was also used to transport the tubs of clay. Our job was to maintain the pumps at the bottom of the shaft which kept the pit reasonably free of water. There were tunnels radiating from the base of the shaft, and each tunnel had a pair of rails on which a dobbin full of clay was pulled up. They were pulled up by a compressed-air winch back to the shaft bottom, where the cage would take them back up to the surface. I can recall these trucks coming off the rails and seeing the miners who were stripped to the waist, dripping wet, both with their own sweat and with the water which constantly dripped from the low roof. The clay was grey, with streaks of yellow-brown, and no matter whether it was wet or dry, there was always water around. This mixed with the clay and made a rich creamy yellow substance which covered everything and everybody. Into this environment was added thick black smoke from the kilns for, as was often the case, coal was also mined here. This fuelled the kilns and burnt quite inefficiently, hence the black smoke.

A miner would crouch down with his back against the dobbin and, with a grunt and a large intake of air, would heave one corner of the dobbin back onto the rail. After sloshing about for some time, we would release the pump and take it and ourselves up top, to examine it and try to put it right. On the top of the bank the dobbins of clay were rolled along until they arrived at the mill to be unloaded. The clay mill was a large steel pan about eight feet wide and there were two heavy stone wheels rotating, which were driven from the centre. This pummelled the clay until it could be moulded. It came out of the machine as a large square sausage, and then a wire was drawn across it to cut a measured amount. One of the women would then pick up this gob of clay, hold it head high, and throw it with considerable force into the wooden mould on the table Any surplus clay was then scraped off and after ten of these had been done they were wheeled away to be placed into the kiln. As you can imagine, it was extremely arduous work, and I soon learned not to get in anyone's way. I was young and nervous, and some of the women terrified me. They loved to tease such a shy young lad and I tried to keep out of their way! The bricks produced here were for lining furnaces as firebricks. The church at Quarry Bank was built with these and remains a fine monument to the firebrick makers.

I also worked as a contract electrician at another pit in Lower Gornal which was known locally as "Sam Chaneys, down the alley" — this was a drift pit as against a pit reached by shaft, such as the Hadcroft. The pit was reached by an incline of between one and two hundred yards in length and we walked down into the pit. At the top of the incline stood the winding house, which had an electric winch to pull or lower the dobbins up and down the incline. About a third of the track was above ground, and the remainder disappeared out of view. I can still see it in my imagination. The entrance was about four and a half foot high and of a similar width. One walked in the middle of the track between two steel railway lines on which the coal dobbins ran. The steel tracks had been mounted on wooden sleepers at approximately two foot intervals, and one had to be very careful when walking, putting one's feet either in between or on top of the sleepers. In the centre of the track ran the steel wire hawser that was used to pull up the tubs, and this ran in a groove of its own making. Along one side were a series of posts sprouting out of the ground about four feet high, running from the engine house to where the track disappeared underground. Near the top of the posts were secured two galvanised wires on white porcelain bobbins, which were about a hand's width apart and functioned as the tub signalling system. When the tubs were required to move, the wires were pinched together once, which rang a bell in the engine house to get the appropriate action. As I made my way down, I could hear the bell with varying degrees of clarity. Apart from the bell, there was the wire rope by one's feet, and this would start to move in answer to the signal. Now I really had to keep my wits about me, as a tub would soon be passing. The direction was indicated by the rope, and it was certainly no place for day-dreaming. Whilst above ground you could stand to one side and let the tub safely pass, but below ground it was a different matter. Once underground, one was confined by the sides of the tunnel.

The sides of the tunnel were supported by small pieces of post (which we called trees), six to eight inches diameter in width, with another on top to support the roof. These goalpost-like structures were placed every three foot along the tunnel, with just enough space between them for the dobbins to run through. There was very little space to spare. If you heard a dobbin coming, you moved quickly to a gap on the side and pressed yourself flat against it until the dobbin had passed by — not ideal working conditions! We used candles to work by, for this was a non-gaseous pit, so a naked flame was permitted. As one entered the drift, one picked up a pair of tallow candles and a gob of clay which, when mixed with a little spittle, was formed into a candleholder and stuck onto one of the tree-trunk supports. Another job was to get power from above ground to down in the pit. This involved climbing up a tall post, making the connections into a box, and then an apprentice would pass up boiling hot pitch which was poured into the box to seal it and make it weatherproof. I still have the scar on my hand where, one Christmas Eve, my apprentice was careless passing the pitch up to me and I burnt my hand!

One of the unusual places where we worked was Ridges in Shaw Road, Dudley. This was a glue factory and they used to boil animal bones to make the glue — the stench was terrible, but it was all grist to the mill.

Whilst I was in the army Laurie had started courting Margaret Round, who was always known as Peggy. She called him Bill, from his second name of William, and from that time on he was known to everyone as Bill. Jean and I were still courting. On the 8th October 1949, Jean and I were married at St Paul's Church, Tipton. I was twenty, and she was to be twenty-two two days later. I had to get my parents' permission to marry because I was under twenty-one! We went to

Bridlington for our six-day honeymoon, where we stayed with my cousin Harold and his wife Cath. I had only managed to save eight pounds so we had to be careful, but we enjoyed ourselves. Harold was a coach driver, so he took us to some local beauty spots and we visited the Goose Fair at Hull, as well as Flamborough Head which was one of my mother's favourite spots. In those days Bridlington was a quiet, basic seaside town with very few amusements. I was most surprised to see how it had altered when I visited the town in 1998.

When we returned to the Midlands, we lived for a time with Jean's parents in their council house in Tipton. I built a shed there, and helped Jean's father in the garden. He was a short, tubby, happy man who worked as a crane driver, but I didn't get on with my mother-in-law; she was a very hard woman. It became difficult for us to continue living there, and we moved to live with Jean's sister May and her husband Glenn in Woodsetton. We rented the front room, and bought ourselves a bed-settee. In May 1951 I changed employment again, became an electrician at Ocker Hill Power Station, and bought a 97 cc auto cycle to travel there and back. Ocker Hill was a large power station of a hundred megawatt capacity. I was soon working on high tension switch gear and transformers. It was an unusual power station, for the cooling towers were built in such a manner to give room underneath for workshops, battery rooms and switchgear. This was a coal-fired station with steam boilers to feed the turbines. It was here that I did my first invention. We had to put one thousand watt screw-bulbs in lamps twenty foot high up in the roof of one part of a huge fan room. There was very little support for the ladder (just a very narrow metal ledge), and it was a very precarious business to get up there and deal with the bulb, which was huge. I was never very good at heights, so very quickly decided that there must be a better way to deal with this problem. I made a fifteen-foot tube with a remote handgrip to hold the six-inch diameter bulbs, and a lever to operate it at the other end. This worked well unless the bulb broke in the lamp holder. However, to deal with this contingency, I put on the opposite end to the hand a rubber plug with a left hand thread. I could then safely remove the old brass cap and then put the new bulb in, all from the safety of the floor! I received a princely five pounds for this invention, but of course I didn't patent it as I knew nothing about patents and idea protection in those days. When the plant was busy making electricity, we were unable to do much maintenance. I would go on the diesel locomotive and play chess with the driver. As you can imagine one couldn't play normal chess in the cab, so I designed my own vertical chess board which we could hang in the cab — the chess men were then hung on pegs on the face of this chess board.

Bill and Peggy married in 1952, and Peggy worked as a shop assistant at Wyse Radio until the boys were born. They had two boys, Graham and Martin. Jean and May both worked at Newey's, a factory which made zips, hair grips, press-studs and pins. May was a forewoman and Jean inspected that their zips came up to quality control. One of Jean's friends at the factory had a caravan at Stourport, and Jean and I had some very happy times staying there. We sometimes borrowed their tandem, and rode together along the river bank. Jean had a miscarriage whilst we were living with May. She was quite ill and was taken by ambulance to Queen Elizabeth's Hospital, Birmingham. I will never forget the wonderful care and kindness she had from a red-haired Irish nurse who helped us both with our loss. In 1952 we moved back to Dudley to try to improve our lives and went to live with my parents at Castle Street, where we had the top floor room. Obviously it was now too far to travel to Ocker Hill, so once again I was looking for a new job, eventually finding one as an electrical supervisor. It was whilst we were living here that Jean became pregnant with Rita and gave up work. Rita was born on 3rd May 1953, and Jean and I were thrilled with our little daughter. I bought a Norton Big 6 motorbike with sidecar on hire purchase so I could transport my small family. I managed to get hold of a Perspex dome from the cockpit of a fighter plane — there were a lot of scrap-parts after the war. I heated this up, moulded it and made a cover for the sidecar; it was great. I can remember driving us to Swanage for a short holiday in a caravan, and can also clearly recollect my dismay when I was once overtaken by one of the wheels which had come off! My parents bought a ten-inch television from the Midlands Electricity Board on hire purchase, so that we could all watch the coronation of Queen Elizabeth; we watched avidly. People were so much more patriotic in those days. We were still using our bed settee, and one morning we were hurrying to tidy the room up when we realised we'd lost Rita — only to find, to our horror, that we'd folded her up in the bed-settee when we'd closed it. Fortunately she survived our early parental mistakes unscathed!

When Rita was a year old, we found a small cottage for sale at St Luke's Terrace, Dudley. It cost two hundred and fifty pounds. I had to borrow two hundred pounds from my mother-in-law, and she came round every Friday afternoon to collect two shillings and sixpence. It was a very basic cottage, on the bank of a coal yard with a ten-foot drop down to a rail line, and was in quite a state. When we got the key, there was still a bed in the bedroom with a half-filled used chamber pot under it! I spent the first week we moved building a wall to block off the drop so that Rita could play safely. I'll always remember that it was early May, but it was so cold that it actually snowed whilst I was working! There was a tiny sitting room and small kitchen downstairs, and two small bedrooms upstairs, with an Elsan toilet outside. I put an Ideal stove in the kitchen and ran hot water to one of the upstairs rooms so that we could have a bath. Jean had several early miscarriages here, and was never very strong. We also had our first dog, a little black Scottie, one of several dogs we had during our marriage.

About this time I went to work for Babcock's and Wilcox, a very large firm of boiler makers. They needed electricians to go "crack-detecting" at new power stations. This was in the days before x-rays or scans were used industrially, and it was a method used to detect any cracks when the large steel pipes were welded together. It was essential that any leaks were discovered before the high-pressure steam was let through. I was sent to Ince power station on the River Dee near Liverpool to do this job. We had to wind either side of the welded pipe with coils of heavy wire, then paint on iron filings and printers ink onto the weld. We then supplied heavy electrical current to the wire, effectively making it into a magnet. If there were any holes in the weld, it would show in the alignment of the iron filings. We then wrapped a sheet of paper round this, and it printed out a permanent record.

While I was away, our little dog was run over by a brewer's dray and killed. We hadn't had it long and Jean was understandably very upset. The firm wanted me to travel all over England, but I realised that this wasn't possible with a wife and young child to care for. My father and Bill suggested that I try to find work at Round Oak Steel Works, where they were both then working. I was lucky enough to find employment there. I was taken on as a charge hand in the motor generator house. This was just being commissioned so it was a good time for me to start there. Bill was shift electrician, but he fell asleep during a quiet period; unfortunately he was discovered and got the sack. He moved on to Bilston Steel Works, and my father retired not long after I started. I soon realised that my new job at Round Oak was the best move I could have made, and I was extremely happy there.

CHAPTER
SIX

We lived at St Luke's Terrace for nearly two years, when Dudley Council decided they wanted to develop the site, and put a compulsory purchase order on the house. They gave us four hundred pounds, and we were able to rent a council house at Copse Rd, on the Saltwells Estate. Rita was now three, and I was able to swap the motor-bike for an old Ford van. A little later we moved again, on the same estate, to Ashfield Crescent, and I was able to buy a smart A35 van, which was my pride and joy. Bill had been on holiday in Blackpool with his family and had a very nasty accident when his young son jumped on him, rupturing his spleen. After his operation, he was sent to a Union convalescence home in Weston and I was able to drive there in my van to bring him back to Dudley.

By this time my parents had also moved to a council house on the same estate. Rita started school at Dudley Wood Primary School. In her second year she broke her leg very badly. I can remember making her a red and black trolley so that she could keep her toys near her. Jean had to take her back to hospital quite often to have the plaster renewed. One of Rita's vivid memories is of her mother taking her to Brierley Hill after each hospital appointment, to buy her an outfit for her Cindy doll — a reward for being brave. At that time the company was offering its employees a chance to buy a plot of land in Mill Street, Brierley Hill. A plot was going to cost three hundred pounds and we decided to buy one and build a house, which has always been a life-long ambition of mine. I went to look at a self-build scheme in Kingswinford and was extremely keen. I started saving for the deposit, though I was working such long hours I don't know when I would have ever had time to build it!

At the time I didn't realise that because I was ambitious and needed to make a living, that this sometimes came at the expense of my family life. Jean was very often lonely, her nerves were bad and, in hindsight, I am afraid there were times when I never really understood or made allowances for her feelings. Like many people, I found it difficult to understand mental illness; I think I would have been more understanding if it had been something visible, like a broken limb. Things came to a head when Jean took an overdose of sleeping tablets. It was really a cry for help, and I had to make some changes. When Jean came out of hospital she was still suffering problems with her nerves, so I was anxious to move to a better area to help with her recovery. As I'd had a promotion, we decided that if I sold my beloved A35 van and used the deposit I'd already saved for the self-build, we should have enough to move from the council property to a new semi-detached house at Marlow Close, Netherton. The house cost two thousand, three hundred pounds and the mortgage interest rate was then six per cent, which was quite reasonable, so we could just about afford it. The company paid to install a telephone so that I could be called out at any time in case of emergencies. I now felt things were looking up again.

This move gave Jean a new start and it did help considerably. However, she then started a compulsive obsessive disorder, which made life very difficult. I was working very long hours as well as being called out at night-time. Jean would take all the tins from the cupboard; polish them before returning them to the cupboard, and then start again. Rita was only ten at the time, and at school, but would encourage her mother to do this once and then distract her to do something else. I have always been so grateful that Rita was able to help Jean in this way. Life settled down. Rita thrived at school and was a lovely child. She can remember me taking her to Round Oak to show her where Daddy worked and how the steel was made. She can very distinctly remember the heat and the steam, and also the mess room with its smell of old boots and oily overalls. She recalls standing on a pedestrian bridge over the roller tracks which carried red-hot glowing pieces of steel, a dramatic introduction to the steel works; it must have looked like Dante's Inferno to a child!

We now got ourselves another dog, a corgi called Scamp. He was rather sharp and you had to watch out for nips! We wanted a kennel for him in the garden so, ever inventive, I brought home a large, empty wooden barrel from work and converted this into his kennel — complete with window! Jean was so much happier at

Marlow Close. She was within walking distance of Cradley Heath, so could easily get to the shops, and would walk to meet me after I'd been paid on a Friday night. She would often potter in the garden with me and would sometimes get the bus to Dudley, and then I'd pick her up and bring her home. Life was really looking up; I had a wonderful wife, a lovely little daughter, a decent home, and a job I loved.

When I started working at Round Oak Steel Works, I began by working in the Motor Generator House which supplied the heavy duty DC power for the heavy mills. I was fortunate starting when I did, as the new generation plant was just being commissioned. It ran twenty-four hours a day, with a shift electrician in attendance. When I got to know more about it, I was made charge-hand on days. I found it fascinating learning how the steel was made. Firstly, in the melting shop hundreds of tons of scrap steel were put into furnaces and melted until it became liquid. This was then run off into giant ladles, something in the order of fifty tons at a time. These ladles were carried by overhead cranes, and dispensed the molten steel into giant lollipop-shaped moulds, each with a capacity of four to five tons. These stood in groups of four on a low railway wagon until the steel solidified, and were then transported by rail to the cogging mill area, where the ingots were stripped from the mould and put into soaking pits. These were under-floor furnaces which kept the ingots at a temperature suitable for rolling. The drive motor for the cogging mill which dealt with the ingots was four thousand horse power, which was controlled by a driver who could watch the rollers and alter the speed from nought to six hundred rpm, and then back in reverse, to squeeze the steel smaller as it went through backwards and forwards. There were three huge adjustable rollers which would squeeze the soft ingots, which were eighteen inches square, until they became four or five inches square and elongated to about thirty or forty foot long. This was done with a comparatively small joy stick; it was amazing to watch as the ingot travelled slowly backwards and forwards through the revolving rolls. As the ingot bit between the rollers, a shower of sparks, steam and noise drowned the place. By the very nature of the heat used, the rollers had to be continually sprayed with water, so the combination of the water and heat brought about this steam. Further down the track, whilst they were still hot, the newly formed billets were cut into suitable lengths and transported by crane to the Heavy Mills, which was adjacent, or by rail across the road to Level St Mills.

I had only worked at Round Oak for about six months when I was made a chargehand. This was a good promotion, and I was now working days. About a year later I was asked to go across the road to the Level Street Mills, as the electrical foreman was retiring in the near future, and I would eventually be promoted to foreman, which was a huge responsibility, a great step forward in my life. As you can imagine I was very excited. All the equipment at Level Street Mills was very sophisticated, with complicated electrics, and I realised this was going to be quite a challenge.

Let me give a general description of the Level St Mill before I go any further. The job of the mill was to convert the steel billets which were approximately fifteen foot long, four to five inches square, into customer-suitable lengths of angle, round, square etc and into sizes up to a hundred feet long. The billets arrived from the Top Works on specially designed rail wagons. They were unloaded by large cranes which had an electro-magnetic pick up, to put them into a storage bay that was en-route to the oil-fired furnace, where they were once again fired up to red heat. I can very clearly remember, even after all this time, an incident which happened when we had to replace one of these crane motors. They were extremely heavy, about a ton each in weight, and were situated about forty feet above the ground. One of the motors was faulty, and we had to bring it down with chain and block tackle, and then haul a new motor up to take its place. I was in charge, and failed to notice one of the men had used the incorrect steel sling, so that when we started hauling it into position, the fixings snapped and the motor crashed down, right on top of the spare motor we were going to repair. What a panic ensued! We had to borrow a spare motor from English Electric, and I was severely reprimanded — which was fair enough, it was my responsibility to see that all went smoothly.

The billets were all laid side by side at the rear entrance to the furnace, and as a hot one was required at the front, a pair of electric rams pushed a load of bars slowly forward, so that one would slip out hot at the other end. It was so hot there, we used to bake potatoes on the outside of the furnace! One of my jobs was to organise the water-cooled cameras which looked into the inside of the furnace. The rams were operated by a woman in a glass cabin overseeing the loading of these billets. She had a small television screen which showed the inside of the front of the furnace, so she knew as one was going out. When she received a signal, she operated a lever to work the rams.

The hot billet which left the furnace then dropped onto electrically driven rollers that were also controlled by an operator — usually women, who were sited in glass "pulpits" above the rolling mill. They were able to manipulate the sideways movement of the billets on the rollers. The billets were then squeezed through the rollers to perhaps ten per cent smaller. The billet then continued to another set of rollers about thirty yards on, and would again be squeezed until they were reduced again, and yet again, varying in shape according to the end product. On the way a billet would go through six sets of rollers, each reducing it by a small amount until it became the required product and ended up at its resting place on a cooling bank. From the furnace to the cooling bank was effectively a continuous track, so if there was a problem with anything en route, the metal cooled and could go no further as the rollers were only capable of dealing with hot metal. All the electrics were monitored with rolling charts that looked similar to seismographs that record earthquakes. They were used to see the start and stop, and also volume of current and usage time. In those days I didn't have to wear glasses, and I remember an electrician coming to me and saying that the recorder pen nib was blocked. I was positive that there was no blockage, so I pulled a hair from his head and threaded it into the tiny nib to prove it wasn't blocked — point made! The organisation of planned maintenance to avoid problems later has stood me in good stead for the rest of my life.

Another lesson I learned was when I had been called out one night, as there was a major problem and my boss and all the mill chiefs were there. The mill had been stopped for over an hour, and they were going to start it up again when I shouted, "Stop!" as I'd seen a problem. My boss said, "Len's right, he's in charge here, anyone can say stop." After further checks on my recommendations, the fault was cured and the mill started up again. After that I was never again frightened to say "stop" when necessary, and often quote this incident.

The problem was that if anything electrical went wrong at any stage, it stopped the whole process and everything in the mill was brought to a standstill. There were two electricians on each shift, but they needed help on occasions. The main control board was an impressive black slate eight foot tall and one hundred yards long covered with switches and relays. This controlled four or five 4000 horsepower, 600 volt DC motors. It was for this equipment that I designed a flow chart fact-finding book. If there was a problem, the electrician on duty could look at the chart to locate the problem: "If x relay doesn't close, go to y or push z". It was a good system and saved me getting out of bed unnecessarily. I had some time on shifts as well as days, learning the intricacies of the job, and then was on days only, had my own office, and was paid monthly.

At one time the electricians called a strike. There were about one hundred electricians, and apart from the cogging mills, heavy mills and Level St Mills, there were two melting shops, the arc melting shop and the open hearth melting shop. The buildings covered about five square miles. There were fifteen foremen who had to try to cover all the electricians' work over the twenty-four hours for seven days. Each one of us had twelve hours on and twelve hours off, with two of us on at a time. When I got home, my feet were bleeding due to the tremendous amount of running around I was doing, both on the level and up on top of cranes. We all felt very satisfied at the end of the strike that we had kept the place going.

Whilst I was at Level Street, I had a hobby making wrought iron. I made various things for friends and paying customers. I even repaired my kettle at work, giving it a wrought iron handle! I was featured in our work's magazine. Quoting from the article: "It's said a change is as good as a rest, and Len Cruddas has found this to be true, turning from looking after complicated electrical gear problems of a giant rolling mill to the manipulating of cold strip into a variety of shapes by hand or wrought iron work. Len has made many attractive chandeliers, house names, tables, etc for his friends". I found most of my spare time was taken up making these wrought iron items, and the extra money certainly helped.

Rita moved to Saltwells Secondary Modern School when she was eleven. Jean was still unwell, and it was a great blessing that Rita was such a support to her. I was working extremely long hours and was totally wrapped up in the business. We went for our first holiday abroad, on a package tour to Spain; I remember it only cost twenty-eight pounds! I had very little time for hobbies, apart from the wrought iron, but I did enjoy spending any spare time I could find working in the garden. I built a zigzag path which amused Rita and her friends, and also enjoyed growing chrysanthemums in my greenhouse.

My brother Bill was working at Stewart & Lloyds Steel Works, Bilston, but in 1965, he was on strike. He was filling in his time doing electrical work and soon had too much work for one person, so I went to help him in my spare time. Eventually we contemplated the possibility of making a partnership. I consulted various people, including my boss. He was very helpful as he told me I could never progress any further in the company without a degree. So, after ten happy years at Round Oak Steel Works, I left and Bill and I started Cruddas Electrics. Within the next five years one heard rumours that Round Oak was to close, and sure enough it did, bringing an end to a great industrial heritage.

The shopping centre, Merry Hill, now stands on what used to be Merry Hill Farm and Round Oaks. It seems so strange to stand in Level Street and look down over the shopping centre. I try to explain to my wife and grandchildren where the steelworks stood. I suppose everything changes, and the area is certainly pleasanter and greener nowadays. Grass banks and islands of flowers are sited where the trains ran carrying the steel and the slag. At night the sky was bright red with orange smoke above when the hot slag was tipped down the bank. It could be seen for miles; now the lights at night are from the shops, restaurants, bars and night clubs.

CHAPTER
SEVEN

Both Bill and I were experts at repairing magnetic cranes, so in between doing domestic electrics we were looking after the magnetic cranes in Pear Tree Lane scrapyard. The owner, Ted, gave us the use of a large corrugated steel building as part payment for our work, so we were able to keep our electrical equipment in there. We also started making small wrought iron items. The electrical work grew from maintaining these cranes and automatic lathes to overhead cranes. These were at Stourbridge Stockholders and were over the tops of acid baths. These acid baths were used to immerse steel plates to clean the scale from them. If the cranes broke down, they had to be repaired very quickly or the steel plates would be damaged. It was quite hair-raising, working high above the acid baths with no safety equipment; it amazes me that so many of the jobs I've done wouldn't now be allowed under Health & Safety regulations. We gave a very good twenty-four hour service, and the money was quite good. However, we were unable to find any decent electricians to employ and we only had two pair of hands between us, so the busier we got, the harder life became. We moved to another building, in Station Road, Cradley Heath, and

69

employed two men to make wrought iron gates. We could teach this trade quickly, unlike the complex electrics, but the electrics had earned us good money with our twenty-four hour call out.

Jean and I went out with Bill and his wife Peggy most Wednesday nights. We'd go to a pub and Bill and I would play darts together. One weekend we all went off together for a break in Weston-Super-Mare where, by a strange co-incidence, we came across a shop selling nothing else but wrought iron. This gave us some food for thought. We discussed the possibility of us doing something similar ourselves, and within a month we had rented a small shop in Cradley Heath and called it "The Wrought Iron Shop". We had a telephone extension to our little workshop in Station Rd and gradually gave up the electrical business. We boasted that we measured, made and fitted all our jobs, and the work poured in. We had to take on another two men to cope with it. We made security grilles, bars and gates, industrial and commercial as well as domestic. Within about twelve months we had outgrown our factory and had to move to Tividale, which was about five miles away. This enabled us to increase production and to open a separate paint shop. We employed a lady called Betty Green to look after the shop and also to do the office work in Cradley Heath. We started to do a lot of work for the local builders, and changed our name to Cruddas Ironcraft.

Because of the five miles distance between the works and the shop we had to do a lot of chasing about, and I soon knew the West Midlands extremely thoroughly.

There was a little bakery in Smethwick where they baked the most delicious cream éclairs. If I was passing, I'd call in to buy some, and then ring Jean from a call box (no mobile phones in those days!) to say, "Put the kettle on, darling, I'm on my way home with some cakes". We were so busy I would work every Sunday, travelling around, measuring and selling wrought iron throughout the West Midlands; Jean would often come with me, and we would have as many as twenty calls on a Sunday.

In 1969, an empty chain works opposite Cradley Heath Library became vacant, and was up for sale at thirteen thousand pounds. By then we had saved some money, but not enough to buy these premises. I was determined to have them by hook or by crook, as I could see the potential. Bill was doubtful at the time, and I can remember telling him that we were looking at our future pension! We went to see the manager at Lloyds Bank, who was a friend, but we hadn't got enough collateral. He suggested we went to Nat West and introduced us to the manager there, a Mr King, and he came to see the property. He was impressed with the site and agreed with me that it had great potential, but couldn't lend us the full amount we needed. He suggested we talked to the vendors and we came to an amicable arrangement. We had two or three thousand pounds for the deposit, the bank lent us four thousand pounds and the vendors allowed us to pay the remainder over the next four years. We committed ourselves to this, and in fact we paid it all off in less than the four years.

The property was about three quarters of an acre overall. There were twenty blacksmiths' hearths with anvils, which had been in existence for the last one hundred and fifty years. We used one of these with a fake sword in it at the front entrance. The sword didn't last intact for very long before vandals broke it off. Not to be defeated, we made a new sword out of a steel car spring, and recessed and welded it into the anvil, and this lasted for another thirty years! There was also a large chain-testing building which was more than a hundred yards long, where steel chains were stretched to breaking point to test their strength. There was an office block that was also the same age, with upright desks and high stools where the clerks used to sit, writing up all the certificates for the chain. The bottom of this office block was part of the stores; there was also a weighbridge and stables. The floors were going rotten and there were signs of rats, but this wasn't a concern to us, we knew we could do most of the work required ourselves. We rented out one unit as a carpenter's shop, and then converted the long building into a factory for the manufacture of wrought iron, with eight benches, welders and all the necessary equipment. We put in a new paint shop with an underground pit, where all the gates which were not galvanised were dipped into red oxide.

The electrics all had to be re-wired, and this was a major job. Fortunately we were both good with our hands and were able to undertake nearly all of the work ourselves. Gas had to be installed for heating, and the glass panels in the roof of the chain-testing shop which were in a dangerous condition had to be replaced. These panels were about thirty yards long and four foot wide. Bill and I worked at weekends replacing the glass with translucent fibreglass panels which were very successful. We altered the bottom floor of the office block into a retail shop, store, kitchen and offices for ourselves. We also had to alter the front of the building to give us a retail shop and display windows, and after some consultation with the planning department of the local council we were able to go ahead with our plans.

We were now able to give up the rented shop and bring the business under one roof. I was doing most of the sales whilst Bill was sorting the factory out. Once we were settled in and in production, we soon had the first floor available to rent. A small company who made ladies' underwear approached us, and we rented this space for their sewing machinists. At this period in time we invested in advertising in the Yellow Pages, which was new then. We were the only people in the area doing ironcraft, so we started that section in the directory — now there are many firms advertising wrought iron! We gradually altered more of the buildings into separate units, so were able to rent out several more, and in the end were receiving eleven thousand pounds a year rent, but we were always very choosy about our tenants. I never allowed car repairs or anything I felt would be detrimental to the property.

Rita would come into the office on Saturdays or after school to help Betty. She left school when she was fifteen and as she was very keen to be a window-dresser, she started work at Beattie's, the department store in

Dudley. Rita was an extremely pretty young lady; in our Yorkshire vernacular I'd say "She'd fetch ducks off t'watter!" Parents often have problems with such attractive daughters, and I've heard terrible stories from other parents, but Rita was never any problem to us. She met Robert about this time, and I had a job to believe he was only sixteen — he was a big lad, and looked a lot older! When we first moved in we found the mains waterpipes were leaking and we had to replace the pipes from the road for fifty yards into the yard. Robert would come in at weekends and dig the trench for this. It was a big job, and kept him busy for quite a few weekends!

Rita and Robert started seeing each other seriously and went regularly to the Plaza dance hall in Oldhill. We often watched Match of the Day together on Saturday nights, as Robert enjoyed football. The only time I ever went to a professional football match was when I went with Robert to see Wolverhampton play Leeds. Robert went to Manchester University to take an engineering degree, and Rita left Beattie's and came to work at the Wrought Iron Centre. It was about this time that Bill's eldest son Graham left school and also came to work in the family business. Robert and Rita became engaged and on 26th July 1974, they were married by the Rev. Crisp at Dudley Wood. They found a little terraced house in Compton Road, Cradley Heath, and Jean and I helped them to buy it by giving them a small deposit. I helped Robert get the house ready for them to move in, teaching him the ins and outs of electrical house re-wiring!

We slowly enlarged our range of products at the Wrought Iron Shop. We proudly boasted that we kept a thousand gates in stock. During quiet periods we would put the lads on bonus, making up gates for stock. There were four basic stock designs, The Abbey, Cathedral, Minster and Priory. Our aim was to satisfy the majority of customers with the minimum of problems. Easy fitting was achieved rather cunningly by using auto latches, which had not been used previously for iron gates. We used the fixed portion of the latch, so that a peg could be adapted to any length and the single and side gates were made in three-inch increments, from two foot three inches to three foot nine inches, which could then be further adjusted by the pin and hinge arrangement. We used short, normal and long hinges and this combination gave us tremendous versatility. We increased our range of products by supplying and fitting security grilles, railings, hall furniture, room dividers and sun canopies. We then went on to make spiral staircases, fire escapes and specialist iron work to architect's drawing, even exporting to Jamaica and France. I'd perfected a method of producing wrought iron spiral staircases which made them much easier to assemble. We also produced white nylon-coated stair units in varying sizes to replace the wooden uprights in houses which had been built in the twenties and thirties. I had small pieces of the nylon-coated steel made into key fobs, and would send them out with a quote, to show the quality of our material. We advertised the stair units in the *Reveille* newspaper (now defunct) and we were selling in excess of one thousand pounds a week by mail order, which was very good money in those days. We thought of opening another shop in Birmingham or franchising the business, but found as partners it was difficult to agree on the way forward.

Always a big believer in publicity, we would often write signs on the window incorrectly spelt, people would come into the shop to educate us — and leave after buying something! Once I even hung a dummy's legs out of a top window — that caused some interest! We always made sure we got plenty of coverage in the local press, particularly when we got a large or interesting order — free publicity is life blood to a business. The local council was a major employer. We tendered for many jobs, from the railings and decorative ironwork at Oldbury Council Offices, to balconies and railings at council housing estates. We also were responsible for a great deal of lighting fittings ordered by local breweries for pubs which were being renovated, and also for decorative screens and fittings in restaurants and bars. There was quite a demand at that time for wrought iron fittings to hang up the glasses above the bar, and we designed and made many of these. I remember designing some very decorative panels for an Italian restaurant in Stourbridge. I drew out Mediterranean scenes, such as the Bridge of Sighs, which were then cut out of light steel, and fitted into internal arches. They were very attractive, and the owners were so pleased with them that they had them photographed for the local press. We also did a lot of work at hotels in Birmingham; one of these was to make the steel safety railings at the Swallow Hotel as the original ones didn't meet safety requirements.

I started to get interested in computers in the 1980s. My first computer was an Apple, and before long I had got into programming this. I worked on a programme for the shop, where the customer's requirements would simply be typed in and a print-out would result with the full details, time required, weight, price etc. As you can imagine, with such a range of products available, this took me many, many hours. Often Jean would wake up, and call out, asking me "to give up, Len, please come to bed!" The programme turned out to be very useful for quotations and sales and helped the staff for many years. I'd thoroughly enjoyed working on it, and realised that I would have loved a career as a computer programmer. How lucky youngsters are nowadays — they have so many more career choices than we had.

After Rita's marriage Jean and I found a bungalow which we both liked in Olive Hall Road, Blackheath. It had been empty for some time, and needed a lot of work doing to it, which was ideal — I've always enjoyed working with my hands, and also relished new projects. I re-wired the property, had a brick arch made as a feature between the lounge and dining room, had central heating installed, and replaced the old broken windows with new bow-fronted windows. Then I built a conservatory right across the back of the house, and a garage with a greenhouse behind it. I had a gas-heater for the greenhouse and grew many fuchsias and large chrysanthemums. We had a productive vegetable garden, and also loganberries and raspberries. There were several fruit trees in the garden, apples, pears and cherry, which made an ideal location for a swing for the grandchildren when they came along.

My sister Marlene married, and after she left home my parents moved to a block of flats in Netherton where they lived until my father died in 1975. Dad was only 67 when he died, so didn't enjoy a long retirement. After Dad died, my mother moved to Cherry Tree Court in Wollescote, to a ground floor flat that was easier for her to manage. About this time, I was busy in the office when Jean rang. She told me she felt ill, and then there was a noise as she collapsed onto the hall floor, still holding the phone. I shouted to Betty to call an ambulance, jumped into my car and raced home, my heart pounding. Jean was taken into hospital with heart problems, but the doctors seemed to be having problems diagnosing her properly and she was discharged. I was extremely worried and wrote a letter to the consultant, expressing my concerns. Jean was by nature very timid and she didn't want me to make a fuss, telling me she felt better and asking me to leave well alone. However, in retrospect, I now realise I should have insisted on her having more investigative treatment.

CHAPTER
EIGHT

In June 1978, Rita and Robert moved to a larger house in Sydney Road, still in Cradley Heath, and in May the following year Jean and I took Rita and Robert on a holiday to America. We flew from Birmingham to what was then Kennedy Airport, and spent three exciting days in New York. Rita and Robert went to the top of the Statue of Liberty — we didn't! We went to the Empire State Building, and visited the ill-fated World Trade Center before travelling by coach to Philadelphia, stopping at hotels at each stop. We saw the Mayflower landing site, where the Pilgrim Fathers first landed in America, Cape Cod and Boston, ending up in Washington DC where we visited the Space Centre. We then returned to Kennedy Airport for the flight home. It's a holiday I've never forgotten, and I shall always be grateful that we had that holiday together

I've another reason to remember that year. In November I had a severe heart attack late one evening whilst watching a film on television. Jean called an ambulance, and I was taken to Dudley Guest Hospital. I can remember being on a bed with a monitor on the bottom of the bed as I was being trundled from one building to another, in the rain. I was later transferred to a hospital at Burton Road and advised to give up smoking — and did so — for a while. My brother persuaded me to start smoking cigars, as he convinced me that they'd be less harmful. Within a short time I was smoking twenty small cigars a day! I had a couple of weeks off work but was soon back in the swing of things again. My heart attack didn't teach me the lessons I really needed to learn — to slow down, take more care of my diet, and above all stop smoking.

When my mother was seventy-five, we had a party for her at the bungalow. We rented a camcorder (they were quite new then and too expensive to buy) and made a video. Rita worked for us until she went on maternity leave in 1979. We were delighted with our new grand-daughter Amy, who was born in March, and then two years later Rita and Robert had another daughter, Emma. Jean and I also had a new addition to our family — Bassbar Benjamin — our new basset hound — otherwise known as Benji! As we lived in Blackheath and Rita was living in Cradley Heath, Jean had to rely on Rita to take her about because Jean didn't drive, and I was always busy. I know Jean adored her little grand-daughters and got a lot of pleasure from being with them. I find it so difficult to remember much about domestic details; I was so involved with the business that work really dominated my life.

I know that Jean managed to persuade me to take some short breaks and over the next few years we visited Garden Festivals, first at Liverpool, then Stoke, Glasgow and finally Wales. I was recently looking through some old postcards and was surprised to see that we'd also been to Cornwall, Somerset, Hereford and London — I really can't remember those holidays at all. I was probably fretting to get back to work! Although Jean and I enjoyed living in our bungalow at Blackheath, we watched some new bungalows being built nearby by Cox Homes and were very impressed with them. We went round the show house, and really liked what we saw, but they were all sold, so we started looking around. I went to the Planning Office to see what applications had been put in by Cox as I particularly liked their bungalows. At the planning office I found that they had applied to build three bungalows and ten houses on their old yard in Quarry Bank. We got a copy of the plans and I had a good think about it. We found that our bungalow would sell very quickly for thirty-eight thousand pounds, and the new bungalow was going to cost about thirty-six thousand. After some deliberation we put our name down for the largest corner plot.

We watched it being built and were able to choose our own fittings, and have the bungalow just as we wanted it. I built a model of the bungalow and the garden, as the garden was a rather difficult site. There was a very steep bank about fifteen feet from the back of the bungalow. I decided to build a curving yellow brick wall to hold the bank back, to make the garden more acceptable. Robert helped me to dig the ground, and prepare the bank for planting conifers and heather. We moved in to the bungalow in April 1987 and quickly started work getting it to our liking. We chose a green carpet with a white dot design which was laid throughout, and Jean soon had her Old Charm grandfather clock — her pride and joy — in position in the sitting room. We'd decided to have a small sun lounge built at the back of the kitchen, leading out onto the garden, and we were very pleased with the completed job. I agreed with Jean that now we might even manage a proper holiday again. As you can imagine, holidays weren't important to me, but I loved my wife very much and was always proud to take her out and about, and now life seemed to be getting so much easier. The business was doing quite well (even so, I still managed to work seven days a week, many weeks!) and money was no longer a problem.

However, life has an unfortunate habit of catching you unawares, just as everything appears to be running smoothly. Jean had been feeling unwell and complaining of pain in her back. I'd often come home from work to find her trying to put Deep Heat on to her back with a wooden spoon. She was in a considerable amount of pain, and despite seeing the doctor several times, she didn't improve. She was sent for tests, where they diagnosed nothing more serious than a hiatus hernia.

We celebrated Jean's sixtieth birthday on the eighth of October. Rita and the family brought a cake, presents and cards; Jean had such a lovely day, but shortly afterwards she collapsed and was taken to hospital by ambulance. I was getting extremely frustrated as nothing seemed to be happening. She was transferred to the Cardiac ward, where the consultant called me in to explain that her heart was failing and that there was nothing more they could do for her. Jean died on the 13th October, just three days after her sixtieth birthday. We had been married for thirty-eight years and I didn't know how I was going to live without her, she had been such a large part of my life. I went back to work and shut myself away, printing thousands of catalogues just to keep busy and to try to forget. I really don't want to remember that period; I was so lonely, lost and unhappy. I know Rita and Robert took me away with them a couple of times in their caravan. We went to London for a short holiday and also spent a week in Scotland. I decided to build a snooker room at the side of the bungalow, just to occupy myself. It was a major undertaking, as it was sixteen foot wide and twenty-seven foot long. When it was finished I bought a red carpet, some leather furniture, an oak corner bar and a full sized snooker table. This project gave me something to do and stopped me brooding.

When the snooker room was finished I had time on my hands, and once again I was finding my loneliness a struggle. I would come home from work, have something to eat, and then sometimes put on a record — Elvis Presley singing "Are you lonesome tonight?" would reduce me to tears — I hated coming back to an empty house; without Jean the heart had gone out of my life and our home had become just a house. I struggled on for a couple of years, but I knew that I didn't want to live alone and I would have to get my life back together, but the problem was — how?

After a lot of deliberation, I finally decided to put an advertisement in the Personal column of the Express & Star, and was very surprised to have thirty-two replies from a wide assortment of lonely ladies! I met several who were very pleasant, but nothing clicked. The last one on the list was Pam; she was blonde, smart and very glamorous, and had been married three times before. I was totally bowled over by her; I couldn't believe my luck, to have such a gorgeous woman in my life. Rita had her doubts, and tried to talk to me about them, but I wouldn't listen, and Pam moved in with me. After she moved in with her poodle, it became clear that we were not really compatible, but because I was in love with her and didn't want to go back to living alone, I struggled to make it work. She was extremely keen to get married, so marriage plans were very soon being made. We were married at the Parish Church of St Mary at Kingswinford in May 1990. It was a very elegant wedding. Pam wore a beautiful long white dress, I had a smart grey suit, and Rita and the girls were pretty bridesmaids in pink. We had a reception in Wordsley, and Pam's family joined us for the festivities. We spent our honeymoon in Wales, and I suppose our problems started straight after this. Our relationship turned out to be disastrous as it very soon became clear that she had lied to me in many ways. She'd professed to like the same music and the same television programmes; now she'd shut herself away in the bedroom each night and ignored me. All the mutual things she had appeared to enjoy with me were now refuted, and each day she'd get a taxi and disappear all day, taking no interest in me or our home. In less than a year the marriage was over; I filed for divorce, which was finalised in 1992. It's strange but I find it very hard

84

to remember much about that period, it seems that my mind blocks out the things that are unpleasant or painful to remember.

Yet again I found my refuge in work, and threw myself into the business. I did meet several ladies, but I was now rather frightened of getting involved. I joined a local club for divorced and widowed people, and started to enjoy some social life. There were parties, visits to the theatre, as well as regular meetings at the Country Club. It was here that I met Ken; his wife had also died, and he'd joined because he was also looking for companionship. He told me that he also belonged to Nexus, a similar organisation. He'd met a lady there called Lorna, who he was sure I would like, and he gave me her telephone number. I rang Lorna on 4th September and we were on the phone for over an hour. We found that we had both been born in Yorkshire, both enjoyed reading and classical music, disliked soap operas, and were both very lonely. Strangely, we were both going away the following day. I'd booked a week's holiday with Saga, cruising on the Rhine, and she was going with Glenda, one of her friends, for a week's holiday in Yorkshire. We got on so well that we agreed to meet for lunch after our holidays. I quite enjoyed my cruise; we flew to Cologne from East Midlands Airport and joined the ship which had about 130 passengers. I quickly made friends with several ladies, who were good company throughout the trip. Next day we sailed for Konigswater, then to Koblenz, passing the ruins of the famous bridge at Remagen which was taken by American troops in 1945. The following days we sailed on to Zell and Alken, past the legendary Lorelei rock near Cat Castle, where they say a beautiful siren used to sit, combing her long hair and luring sailors to their deaths — she wasn't sitting there when we sailed past, although I looked very hard! We visited Rudesheim before returning to Cologne. All along the river we had seen beautiful castles, vineyards and delightful scenery, and I was able to take photographs and also sketch as we went along. Unfortunately I dropped my camera towards the end of the cruise, which was very annoying. We just had time to see the cathedral at Cologne before our flight back home.

A couple of days later I rather nervously turned up on Lorna's doorstep in Worcester to pick her up for lunch. Lorna turned out to be a small, plump lady, fifty-four years old, very easy to talk to, and we got on very well. We had lunch at The Fox just outside Worcester, and then I drove us back to Worcester, where we walked and talked. We visited the Cathedral and had a cup of tea in the café in the cloisters, then walked round the canal and by the river Severn. We told each other about our lives and work as we walked. Lorna worked for British Telecom in Worcester, and had been married for 27 years to a Portuguese when, in 1986, he'd gone to Brazil for a fortnight's business trip — and had not returned! She used to joke that she'd had to wait a long time for some Brazilian coffee and that perhaps he'd been trying to tell her something, but really she had been very hurt by his desertion. Lorna had three grown-up children, Tony, Sara and Elena; she shared a house with her youngest daughter Elena and her young family. I drove Lorna back to her house late afternoon, and we agreed that we'd like to meet again.

Several weeks passed before our next meeting as Lorna had a very busy social life. She was treasurer of her union, secretary of Nexus, the social club she belonged to, and also presented a programme twice a week for Worcester Hospital Radio. However, our next meeting sealed our lives together! We went on a Nexus treasure hunt and I'd arranged to meet Lorna in Kidderminster. She parked her car at the Land Oak, a public house on the outskirts, and I picked her up and drove her to our meeting place, The Falcon in Bridgnorth. We joined some of Lorna's friends for lunch, and Lorna was extremely embarrassed by the inquisition I was given by her friend Pat. Almost as soon as we were introduced, the questioning started.

"Are you divorced or a widower?" she asked.

"Oh, a widower and what do you do?"

"You own your own business — what is it?"

"The Wrought Iron Centre, oh yes, I know that quite well. It's in Cradley Heath High Street, isn't it — with the anvil outside?"

"And where do you live — do you own your home?"

She finally ended up by asking, "And what are your intentions towards my friend?"

Lorna went very red and rushed off to the loo, closely followed by Pat. Pat's husband Tony gave me a wry smile, but offered me no assistance whatsoever. Lorna told me later that Pat had asked what on earth was wrong with her, she'd only been looking after her, and told her, "Now, don't mess around and lose this one — he's nice, he's normal, he's single and he can afford you!!" Pat had been trying to pair her off, but Lorna hadn't felt that she was ready for another relationship; the ending of her marriage had been too painful. Since then Pat and her husband Tony have become extremely good friends.

After lunch we were given our instructions for the treasure hunt and were asked if we minded taking another lady in my car. I know we both feel a bit guilty, to this day, about that poor woman — we were so busy talking and finding out about each other, she was rather neglected. We thoroughly enjoyed ourselves and at the end found that we'd come second, winning a bottle of wine. I suggested to Lorna that she might like to come back to my bungalow for a cup of tea and to see my snooker room — Lorna says that was the most original chat up line she'd ever received! The cup of tea turned into supper, and then we sat listening to music, just feeling very comfortable with each other. We found that we really enjoyed the same music; in fact our collection of compact discs was almost identical! Later that evening I told Lorna I was very attracted to her and her initial reaction was to say that she was frightened of being hurt again. I promised her there and then that I would never hurt her — and fortunately she decided to trust me. Each Friday afternoon from then on I picked Lorna up from her office in Worcester, and we'd spend the weekend together. It was a very special time as we were still getting to know each other. One of our greatest surprises was the depth of love that we had found. I'd known loneliness, and badly wanted companionship, but had never hoped to feel the emotions that now threatened to overwhelm me — it was like being a teenager again! I had certainly never expected to gain such a wonderfully satisfying love life. I know, our children will say "too much information!" but the sheer wonder of it was incredible, and has only grown stronger as we've aged. We went to several parties and shows, but mostly we cooked for each other, then watched a film or listened to music — and talked! I quickly introduced Lorna to Rita and her family. They got on well, but Rita cautioned us to take things easy and not to rush things. I'd always picked up my mother on Sunday morning and cooked her lunch, and Lorna insisted that we kept to the same routine. The first Sunday we picked her up as a couple, Lorna cooked roast beef and Yorkshire puddings. The puddings rose beautifully and Mam said she could tell Lorna was a true Yorkshire woman! Mam's eyesight was extremely bad by now; in fact she was registered blind. She loved to be taken round the garden and would run her fingers over the thymes and lavender, delighting in their fragrance. One day she suddenly asked, "What colour's your hair, Len? I seem to remember it was light brown." I stroked my grey hair ruefully and answered her, "Just remember my hair as it was, Mam."

CHAPTER
NINE

Lorna and I decided to have a week's holiday together, so on 2nd November 1992, we went to the Algarve in Portugal. We'd booked an apartment just outside Vilamoura and it was a magical week. Although it was November, the weather was sunny and the nights balmy, dark and starry. Neither of us felt up to driving in Portugal, so we travelled by bus, and we also walked a good deal. We both enjoyed looking at the architecture; I was fascinated by the wrought iron as well as the Moorish chimneys. We were thrilled with the wonderful displays of exotic flowers, particularly the bougainvillea, hibiscus and succulent, brightly coloured daisy-like flowers. We found a small restaurant where we ate most evenings, sampling sardines and other local food, and afterwards we walked for miles each night after dinner, hand-in-hand under the stars, talking and really getting to know one another. On returning to our apartment, we'd sit outside in the dark on the balcony, watching the night sky, and enjoying each other's company. We went on several excursions; one of these was to see the cork trees and orchards of lemons, tangerines and oranges where we picked fruit from the trees to take home. Then we were taken to a hill top village, where we saw the women doing the washing in large communal stone baths before we had an extremely good lunch in a nearby restaurant. Another trip was a Jeep Safari into the mountains, which was a bit hairy and absolutely terrified Lorna. The drivers raced each other over the bumpy roads and we sat sideways on, with no safety belts! We visited a distillery, high in the mountains, where they made the local "firewater". I reluctantly tried a sip, and felt as if my whole mouth and throat was on fire. Lorna's son Antony was living at that time in the Algarve, with his first wife Caroline and their little daughter, Jacey. They were both working for a time-share company, and were very busy, but we spent some time with them. Antony managed to persuade us to visit the time-share complex, which would help his bonus! The apartments were good quality, but the agents were very hard sell operators and it's easy to see how many people get conned into buying time-share; fortunately we're too level-headed to be taken in! We visited Quarteira, Vilamoura and Loule, packing a lot into our week. I'm usually restless to get back home, but this was one holiday I didn't want to end. I decided there and then that I didn't want Lorna to return to her flat in Worcester, but to move in with me. She agreed, and on our return a week later, Lorna told her daughter Elena, and then we both told Rita — who was not in the least surprised. We stood in front of her, holding hands, and I said that we'd something to tell her. "My God!" she exclaimed, "Don't tell me Lorna's pregnant!" We all laughed, and then she told us that she had been expecting this. Lorna had been rather nervous about telling her mother, Mina, who lived in Jersey. She had good reason; Mina was quite upset about it. "You mean you're going to move in with the man?" she asked, "That's dreadful — to think a daughter of mine is going to live over the brush!" Fortunately Mina soon came round to the fact that we were blissfully happy. Five days later, on Friday 13th November (a date Lorna hated, and hadn't wanted to move on), I picked her up from work as usual, but this time we drove to her home, collected some of her belongings and drove to Quarry Bank to start our new life together.

We shall never forget that first weekend; we were like a pair of lovesick teenagers! Lorna organised her things, and joined the library — very important as she is an avid reader. Mother came for Sunday lunch, and after we'd driven her home I insisted on Lorna driving my car back. She was very reluctant; she hadn't driven an automatic before, and was a bit nervous. However, she soon got the hang of it and enjoyed driving the Rover.

On Monday morning I dropped Lorna off at the station at ten to seven, where she caught the train for work, and drove to the factory. I don't remember much more, just waking up in hospital. Apparently I'd had a heart attack at the wheel of the car. Lorna had only just got to the office and settled down at her computer, when she received a telephone call from Rita, giving her the news. Lorna got a lift from one of her colleagues to the hospital, where Rita met her and told her that I was in intensive care, but conscious and asking for her. She also told her, in no uncertain terms, to look cheerful! It was difficult for her to feel cheerful — I was wired up to various machines, she'd only just moved in with me, and wasn't sure what to do. However, being Lorna, she soon sorted things out. She gave up her various commitments so that she could concentrate on me. It was so fortunate that she felt confident driving my car, as she had to pick it up, and also use it to visit me in hospital. As soon as she was told that I would recover, Lorna bought a rose tree for our garden. It was called Blessings and we always remembered why she planted it.

I was in hospital for five or six days, and was so relieved when they allowed Lorna to take me home. Now I was home I had to take things quietly, and Lorna was still working in Worcester. She left early on a morning, and didn't return until six o'clock at the earliest; the days seemed very long, and I didn't take easily to resting! My daughter Rita worked with me at Cruddas Ironcraft, and soon decided that it was time I retired. I agreed very reluctantly, as she was aided and abetted by Lorna. It felt very strange not to go to work each day. I had been working since the age of fourteen, and the business had become my life. I tried hard to relax, but just two weeks later I was admitted to hospital again for another week or two. Poor Lorna didn't know what she had taken on! They found that a previous heart attack had badly scarred my heart, causing my heart to beat too fast. A cocktail of drugs steadied things down and I started to feel more like my old self.

In the April of that year we went to Jersey for a short holiday, and for me to meet Lorna's mother and family and to attend a family wedding. We had a lovely time, but a phone call from my sister Marlene had us hurrying back. My mother had become ill and had a stroke. We were just in time to say goodbye to her. I've always been grateful that Lorna and Mam had a chance to know and love each other, and that in the short time they knew each other they'd become close.

I was now coming under pressure from all sides to give up smoking. I had smoked since I was a lad, being a regular smoker by the time I was fourteen. Now my cardiac consultant, Lorna and my small grand-daughter Emma put the pressure on me. Lorna had never complained about me smoking, but by this stage I was smoking about twenty small cigarillos a day. She now told me she hated the smell on the furnishings, and was also worried about me. The writing was on the wall! We decided to go to Rhyadder in Wales for a weekend break. I took my largest and finest cigar with me. As we strolled in the twilight I lit it up and informed Lorna that this would be my last cigar. The date was 4th June 1993, and I'm thrilled to say I have managed to keep that promise. Just to make sure I wasn't tempted, Lorna gathered up all my cigars and put them under lock and key in her desk at work! It was very hard at first, and there were times that I must have been unbearable to live with — but gradually the craving ceased, and I am quite sure that I would not be living thirteen years later if I had not made that decision.

I found retirement very hard to come to terms with; I had worked so hard all my life. As you can imagine I was soon scratching my head for ideas to occupy myself. I enjoyed making computer programmes, but I found it difficult to sit in front of a computer screen without a specific project to work on, and I also wanted to use my practical skills again. Lorna and I both enjoyed working together in the garden, so I designed four wrought iron arches going up the steps. We planted thornless roses, ceanothus, clematis, grapes and jasmine to grow over them, and eventually they were quite a picture. I then designed a lean-to greenhouse and Lorna and I built it together. It was an initiation for Lorna, who had by now realised that I always had to be active! Her sister Jacquie came from Jersey for a short visit, and naturally she got roped into helping. It started to rain, but I wasn't going to let that stop work. I rigged up a tarpaulin and set the girls to work under it. Unfortunately it held a huge amount of water, and then deposited it all over them. They gave up work in high dudgeon, changed and decamped to the shops at Merry Hill, leaving me on my own! Lorna chose a peach tree as one of her birthday presents and this went into the new greenhouse. She carefully nurtured it all year, and the following summer we had just one huge peach. Lorna's young grandchildren came to visit, and a small shame-faced Leo came into the house, holding the peach, "Nana, it just camed off in my hand," he explained, so we all had to share it! When the greenhouse was finished, I designed and made a two-seater settee for the sun lounge. Lorna had mentioned several times that we could do with a coffee table in there, but there wasn't the space. My settee had pull out coffee tables and magazine racks built into the arms. I had also designed a surprise feature for Lorna. Knowing she likes to sit with her feet up, I had built in a spring-loaded stool. Lorna had a large collection of ornamental hedgehogs, so I borrowed one to act as the handle for this. When she came home from work I sat her on the sofa, put the little hedgehog in her hand, and ordered her to pull. When she did so, the stool shot out so fast it nearly went through the wall. We laughed until tears were streaming down our faces. Each time we looked at each other or Lorna looked down at the hedgehog, we were off again. It's a wonder I wasn't admitted to the Cardiac Unit again that night.

One Saturday evening we had an unexpected visit from Neil, one of the lads who'd worked for me. He'd come across a group of louts who were tormenting a hedgehog. He'd rescued it and, having seen Lorna's collection of hedgehogs, he'd brought it to us. It was looking very sorry for itself. We put it in a box in our new greenhouse and put down some water and milk. Next morning it looked as if a tornado had hit the place. The hedgehog had climbed on the shelving and knocked over all the plants. We looked up "hedgehogs" on the Internet, and found that they should be fed dog or cat food. We also discovered that one could sex them by holding them in cupped, gloved hands, gently throwing them up into the air, where they would relax, and one could see the sex. I can tell you now — it

96

didn't work! We took the little creature to the vet where we were told it was a male. He wormed and de-flead him, and we christened him Snuffles. He was great fun, but unfortunately our tortoise hated him. The tortoise really belonged to my grand-daughters, but when they acquired a puppy, I had to bring Timmy to live with me — the puppy and Timmy didn't like each other. To amuse the grandchildren I had made Timmy his own bungalow complete with television aerial, and he would put himself to bed in it every night.

After we brought Snuffles back from the vet, we put his box next to Timmy's bungalow. The next morning, Timmy was upside down on his shell with his little legs futilely waving in the air and Snuffles was happily ensconced in Timmy's bungalow! After two more mornings when we had to rescue an indignant Timmy, we resorted to physically putting him in his house, then turning the front against the wall, stopping Snuffles from evicting the rightful resident. Snuffles was a lively addition to our family, but I must admit he was naughty and inquisitive. This was to get him into more trouble. He was investigating a drainpipe when he got stuck and broke his leg. Another expensive visit to the vet followed. The vet was a little worried about operating as he'd never set a hedgehog's leg before — but it went well, and next day we collected a rather dejected Snuffles complete with lightweight cast! He soon regained his confidence, but after a few more narrow escapes (and arguments with Timmy), we regretfully took him to the Hedgehog Sanctuary, where he could be safely put back into the countryside.

I had always been interested in making and inventing things. In our early days at Cruddas Ironcraft I had invented a small gadget which easily and economically made scrolls. At that time I knew nothing about patenting and didn't do anything to protect my idea. Within a short time a German firm had patented a very similar machine and made a great deal of money selling it. Now I had time on my hands, I started looking for solutions to perceived problems — the best way to describe inventions! One of these was the problem of where to keep spare toilet rolls. I flatly refused to have a "crinoline dolly" or the like in the bathroom to hide them, and Lorna didn't like my way of keeping them in a cupboard some way from the bathroom, so the "Popparoll" was born. This was a cylindrical box with a hinged lid, which holds two toilet rolls. It's spring loaded, so when a button is pressed a toilet roll pops out. Yes, I admit that if the button is pressed too hard, the effect can be a bit like the spring-loaded hedgehog! When they were younger, Lorna's two grandsons had many happy times operating it. Lorna and I decided to form a partnership, and called ourselves Cruddas Innovations. We sent off to the Patent Office for their pack on patents, and taught ourselves how to apply for a patent. In due course we applied for one for the Popparoll. I demonstrated it on Channel 4's Big Breakfast show. That was great fun. Lorna and I were taken to London, where we stayed overnight in the Big Breakfast house, and early (very early!) the next morning we were picked up and taken to the Studio for the show. We tried rather half-heartedly to market it, but the gadget never came to commercial fruition; however, our bathrooms and that of the family and friends all sport Popparolls.

About this time I joined the Birmingham Inventors Club. They met once a month at Aston University and I thoroughly enjoyed the meetings. I learned about patents and met other people who were as passionate about innovation as I was. I made friends with several other members who lived locally, and Lorna enjoyed me going as well, as one of the things she missed in our relationship was curry. I can't even stand the smell of curry, so once a month she treated herself to an Indian take-away while I went to the club meeting.

In December 1993 I met Lorna from work as usual when she finished on Friday afternoon. I'd prepared a winter picnic, and drove her to the riverside in Worcester. Once there, despite the mud, I got down on one knee, and asked Lorna to marry me on 15th January 1994. She'd once mentioned that she didn't see herself marrying an old-aged pensioner, so I had booked the wedding for the day before my sixty-fifth birthday — technically I wouldn't yet be a pensioner. I knew that Lorna had been rather worried about the brevity of my previous marriage to Pam. She'd said that she'd felt a little threatened that photographs of my previous wife had shown a slim and glamorous woman. Fortunately my mother and family had convinced her that I had tried hard to save the marriage, and she should have no fears. To my delight, she said "yes" to my proposal, and the next few weeks were busy with making all the arrangements for Christmas, followed by a winter wedding. I had booked the wedding at the Registry Office in Stourbridge. Rita and Lorna went on a shopping trip to find Lorna's wedding dress, the hairdresser was booked, and Lorna's sister Jacquie and her partner Barrie flew from Jersey to attend our wedding. The Saturday morning was cold and crisp. The Registry Office was on top of a multi-story car park — quite depressing. Lorna still teases me about me picking such an unromantic setting!

Jacquie had persuaded Barrie to take her shopping at Merry Hill and was enjoying herself so much that they had to rush to find a taxi to bring them to the Registry Office. The taxi-driver was a Sikh with a large white turban, who didn't appear to know the area, and the car had the exhaust hanging perilously low — the noise as they made their way up to the top floor of the multi-storey was appalling! Sara, Sam and her two boys arrived at the same time as Elena, Mark and their two sons. Sara discovered she had a ladder in her black tights and retreated to the car to change them. Her legs were sticking up in the air, causing a lot of amusement from Saturday shoppers. We were anxiously waiting for Sara to finish dressing and for Jacquie to arrive. The Registrar was getting nervous as there was another wedding taking place immediately after ours. We really thought that we'd have to go ahead without them! Rita, Robert and their two daughters were also at the wedding, along with some of Lorna's friends, Marian and Alan. The ceremony was quite brief, but we were able to take photographs in a pretty roof garden; afterwards we all drove to Page's Restaurant in

Stourbridge for the reception. We'd planned a party at the bungalow that evening, so we went home for a short rest before getting things ready. Unfortunately Lorna's family had to drive back to Hereford with the children so they weren't able to come.

The party was great fun, my daughter and her family came to help, my brother Bill and his wife came, along with our friends and some of Lorna's colleagues from work. Rita and the family had bought us our wedding cake, and the grandchildren took great delight in popping a large balloon filled with confetti over us both. They filmed the wedding and reception, a lovely reminder of a perfect day. The last guests left at nearly three the next morning, so we had a lazy day before catching a train to London where we spent a hectic three-day honeymoon. We stayed in the Hotel Rembrandt in Kensington, which was ideally situated for us to visit the Tate and the Victoria and Albert Museum. We went on a river trip on the Thames to Greenwich, did all the usual tourist things like visiting Westminster Abbey and Covent Garden, and on our last night went to the theatre to see a wonderful performance of *Miss Saigon*. We returned home tired but blissfully happy. We imagined ourselves settling down into a rather boring Darby and Joan existence. Little did we realise how much our lives were to change in the coming years.

CHAPTER
TEN

In May ninety-four we flew to Jersey and hired a car. We spent five days exploring the island and visiting friends and family. Lorna's mother had terminal cancer and was becoming quite frail. However we took her out several times and we enjoyed some pleasant meals together. In August I collapsed and had to be admitted to hospital again. This time I was there for a week and Lorna was getting anxious as Mina was coming to stay with us for a couple of days. Fortunately I was back to my old self before Lorna's brother and his family dropped Mina off. We didn't have a spare room (it was now functioning as the office!) so I made a bed to go in the snooker room, and we really enjoyed her visit. In spite of being in her eighties, Mina was a very pretty lady, bright, articulate and very pithy, a typical Yorkshire lass! It was to be her last trip to England.

That year Lorna and I were considering buying a narrow boat so that we could have short holidays on board. We decided to book a weekend break to see how we got on with the boat. In September we hired a boat from Alvechurch. The autumnal weather was beautiful, and the trees and scenery on the canal were breathtaking. However, we found it quite a physical strain as the boat kept grounding, and the locks were quite hard work. Then quite unexpectedly on Saturday afternoon Lorna had a bad fall. The boat had recently been re-fitted, and they had forgotten to secure the stairs from the cabin to the deck. As she ran up the stairs they moved, throwing her bodily on to the deck and trapping her leg in the rungs of the stairs. She was winded, cut and bruised, and we decided to cut the holiday short and return home. She saw the doctor, who said she was suffering from shock, but otherwise seemed fine. On Monday evening Lorna insisted I went off with my friends to the Inventors' Club, and assured me she'd have a quiet evening at home, enjoying her curry. Just after I had left she started to feel ill. She was clammy, had chest pains and couldn't breathe. The doctor came out to see her and told her it was her gall bladder playing up, and to eat sparingly and to rest. She had been having problems with her gall bladder for a couple of months, so was happy with his diagnosis, and took his advice. I was most concerned when I got back home, but she reassured me, and seemed to improve. Six weeks later she was booked into hospital to have her gall bladder removed. The anaesthetist came to see her, and told her he could not operate as she had suffered a heart attack six weeks earlier! Lorna came out of hospital a couple of days later and soon saw a cardiologist, who told her that the heart was now damaged, and that it had left her with angina. She was prescribed tablets and determined to get on with life. I teased her that she couldn't let me have anything on my own; she even had to have a matching heart attack!

Lorna was still working for British Telecom at Worcester and the daily journey was quite a strain. Her office was about twenty-four miles from Quarry bank and meant a long drive or a train journey. The job had also changed over the years, and had become much more stressful. However, she found someone to job-share with her and started working part-time, which made life much easier.

One of Lorna's jobs at that time was preparing telephone directories. One day she spilt her cup of coffee over her computer keyboard and the proofs she was checking. It did quite a lot of damage, and she was rather upset. I invented a high-sided, weighted coaster, which we called the Drink Station, to prevent this happening again. I begged some drain pipe from a local firm, cut it, made the coaster and painted it. All the family and friends had them for their desks. I put the logo of the pipe firm, with their name and contact details, on to a couple of Drink Stations, and showed them to the firm. To my delight they ordered thirty of them for a Christmas promotion and paid a good price for them. Quite an achievement, as I had got the main material from them gratis!

I carried on going to Birmingham Inventors although it was quite a drive to get there. I met other like-minded inventors, and always enjoyed the meetings. However, several of us were from the Black Country, so I decided to found a local club. We had some publicity in the local press in early 1996, and we soon had phone calls from prospective members. We also got some backing from Sandwell Council, who let us hold monthly meetings at

Oldbury College and provided a secretary, and paid for all the printing, which was a great help.

Amongst our founder members were Jack Blackburn and George Wyers. Jack was in his eighties and quite eccentric. He was a retired architect, with many patents to his name. One of his inventions was the original underfloor central heating concept. Unfortunately he showed this to a rep who was visiting Jack's firm. When he was granted a patent, the rep's firm contested the patent, claiming it had "prior knowledge", and Jack's patent was rescinded, which is quite unusual. As a young man he worked for Sandwell Council. During the Second World War he converted the tyres of his car so that he could drive around the area, operating a stirrup pump, painting the words "Bring on the second front" on to the roads. His boss arrived in the office in a furious mood. "Have you seen what some idiot's writing on the roads?" he asked, and told Jack to arrange to have it removed. Jack very wisely never admitted his guilt. Later in the war, when he was posted to Malaysia and his unit had trouble with termites eating the wooden cabins, he set about filling large bamboo poles with concrete. "That fixed the little blighters, gave 'em toothache!" he told the club. He was the inventor of "concrete grass", now widely used in the building industry to stop tyres damaging turf. It was based on the structure of an egg box and allows grass to grow while being protected from crushing by a concrete surround. He also invented a version of pre-sown grass which he sold to Japan. He was always working on yet another project. Jack was larger than life, bubbling with ideas and great fun. His daughter visited him when he was dying in hospital, and all he wanted to talk about was an invention he'd thought of whilst in bed. When Jack was present we could always be sure of a good meeting. He died in 1998 at the age of 82, a great loss to the club and also to us as a friend.

At that time George still worked as a consultant, designing mirrors for large vehicles, although he too was well over retirement age. He was always entering competitions and won many, many prizes. Sadly George is no longer with us either, as he lost his brave fight against cancer in 2005.

When we founded the club we had assistance from a firm of lawyers who drafted an Agreement for all new members to sign, respecting the confidentiality of all members' inventions — extremely important — and we ensured all potential members signed upon joining. We were a non-profit making organisation, requiring just a small yearly subscription, and were open to anyone with a lively interest in invention and innovation. We very soon had an interesting mix of members, with inventions ranging from the everyday to hair-raising, almost impossible, technology. It surprised us to find how many people didn't know how to protect their ideas or how to even begin to evaluate them. I can remember one young chap who had a totally unworkable idea for which he wasn't able to make a proper prototype, but who was really convinced that companies would fall over themselves to buy. We tried to advise him but inventors are strange beings; we each think our own idea is the best thing since sliced bread, and tend to be very defensive, like a mother with a precious, new-born child! Fortunately, we did have inventors with useful ideas, as well as members with a wealth of skills which they were willing to share. One of our brainwaves however proved to be totally unfeasible. We decided to work on a group project, taking an idea and working on it together — it was a disaster! Inventors tend, by their very nature, to be "loners" and they don't adapt at all well to working with others. As well as the official meetings at Sandwell, we often held impromptu meetings at our bungalow and these were always very lively. In fact Lorna usually had a headache after these informal meetings, the air was so full of ideas, and everyone was laughing and talking — usually at once!

I was still inventing things and my next invention came about because of Lorna. I always say that she provides the need and I provide the invention. We had a fishpond in the garden which used to get covered in blanket weed every summer. Lorna was pulling this out on a stick one morning before going to work and complaining that there had to be a better way of doing the job. By the time she came home from work that night I'd made a prototype weed-collector. Lorna was very impressed with it, and we started to look at ways of getting it made. We quickly came to the conclusion that the cheapest way would be to try to make it ourselves. We applied for a patent — essential with any invention — and over the next few months we had a production line of two working in our garage whenever Lorna wasn't at work. By the time the next spring came, we would be ready to try marketing the Pondwand.

It was about this time that Lorna decided it was time our social life improved, so we joined the University of the Third Age in Stourbridge. We went each week, heard an interesting lecture and then had lunch at the College. I was roped into giving a talk on inventions, and once I'd got over my nerves, I really enjoyed the experience. It was the start of quite a few speaking engagements.

In July 1997 we went with the club for a tour of the Champagne country, based at Rheims. I had never cared for wine but after several days visiting the champagne houses, and tasting their wares, I was quite won over! The guide at one of the champagne houses explained how one of the monks had first discovered champagne. It's said he'd told the other members of his community, "Brothers, I've just tasted the stars". We certainly agreed with him. We also went out for a couple of meals at a local château, and at some delightful little restaurants in the town. I'm a typical Yorkshire man, tending to like my meals plain and simple, very much the roast beef and Yorkshire pudding type! However Lorna has been trying to get me out of my rut ever since she met me, and I have to admit this holiday made me appreciate fine cuisine. It was a very pleasant break, and we brought champagne back to England with us — in fact the coach rattled with the extra bottles we'd all bought. We now regularly have a bottle of champagne as our little treat.

That holiday was the start of some lovely short breaks. We spent a weekend in Buxton, Devon and Yorkshire, and several times we visited Pembrokeshire, Anglesey and Cardigan. We have tried to share our interests; Lorna enjoys visiting stately homes, and beautiful countryside, whilst I prefer to visit more industrial sites. I have to admit she has been quite forebearing, having been taken down a tar tunnel, toured a nuclear power station, and watched replica steam engines working (Trevithick's and Stevenson's Rocket — wonderful stuff!), whilst she has taken me to Chatsworth, the Tate Gallery and numerous gardens. Of course whilst she is enthusing over the beauty of nature I am more often pondering the science behind some building or technical achievement. Lorna was still working part-time, and we couldn't believe how contented we both were with our lot.

One afternoon I received a phone call from Lorna's colleague at work telling me she had suffered a bad angina attack and that they were going to drive her home. I rang the doctor, who asked me to take her to the hospital where they would be expecting her. As soon as Lorna got home, I took her straight to Russell Hall. On the way I suddenly asked Lorna if she found it very hot, and then I started having difficulty breathing. I had to pull over to the side of the road, and Lorna ended up driving us both to hospital! There was a porter waiting for her with a wheelchair, so she asked him to get one for me as well and we were both wheeled into the same bay in Accident and Emergency. As you can imagine the medical staff thought it was quite funny. It wasn't quite so funny when they found my heart was beating incredibly fast. Bells rang and a cardiac emergency team assembled. Lorna was moved to another bay and had a very anxious time while they worked to stabilise me. I was admitted to the Cardiac ward, and poor Lorna had to get herself home. Once again I was in hospital for a week before being allowed home.

In September of that year we entered into negotiations for our Pondwand with Oasis, large distributors. The initial meeting seemed hopeful, and in November we got our first order for a thousand Pondwands. We quickly decided we wouldn't be able to keep up with demand and arranged for them to be made by a local contractor. We also placed some advertisements in water garden magazines and soon had mail orders coming in as well.

In 1998 we were told that Sandwell College had lost its Government funding, and that we would no longer be able to hold our meetings there or have any secretarial support. We desperately started searching for a new venue for the Sandwell Inventors. In April I'd had a small article published in the *Express and Star* about the Round Oak Steel Works that preceded the Merry Hill shopping centre. As a result of this, we were invited to meet with the Administrative Department at Merry Hill. Whilst we were talking, they suggested that we use the Customer Service Suite each month for our club meetings. It was ideal and we quickly changed our name to Black Country Inventors. We were so pleased to have a new venue for the club.

Several people who attended our meetings had paid out good money to companies who offered to "help" inventors. Unfortunately these companies are predators, preying on the inexperienced inventor. We were able to give free advice and, in some cases, stop would-be inventors falling into this trap. I remained Chairman and Lorna was once again Secretary and life was very busy, especially as Pondwand sales were growing.

When I had built the snooker room, I took out the cloakroom to make the entrance to the extension. Lorna had always complained that there was only one toilet in the bungalow. I suggested to her that as I now played very little snooker, it might be possible to alter the room into a bedroom and second bathroom. She was delighted with the idea and we quickly drew up plans for this new project. We decided to do most of the work ourselves. We managed to sell the snooker table and the furniture, and the money we received more than covered our costs. I split the snooker room up into three, a large bedroom, a small dressing room and a bathroom, and decided to make a raised floor so that we could have a sunken bath. It worked very well. There were two steps up to the bathroom from the dressing room. We installed a Jacuzzi in a corner bath, a shower cubicle, bidet, toilet and washbasin. There was an archway to the bathroom, and a smaller arched entrance from the bedroom to the dressing room. We put two small armchairs, a coffee table, a long dressing table, mirror and a music system into the dressing room, and Lorna stencilled the dressing table, archway and curtains with a cornflower and butterfly design on a cream background. We did all the decorating, plumbing and building work ourselves, and it was so satisfying to see the finished product. Finally, I made a large walk-in wardrobe with mirrored doors. There was plenty of hanging space and shelves, and it lit up automatically when the doors opened — Lorna said it made her feel like a film star. Much as I had enjoyed my snooker room, I was the first to admit that the new layout made life much easier, and was a lovely addition to our bungalow. It was well worth sacrificing my snooker table!

The following March Lorna's sister rang to tell us that Mina was dying. We immediately drove to Poole, and got on the ferry to Jersey. We were too late to say goodbye to her. She'd suffered very stoically for several years, and her death was a release from her pain. We stayed for the funeral and all her family were surprised at how many people came to say goodbye to their mother.

On our return journey, Lorna tripped over in the car park whilst we were waiting to board the ferry at Jersey harbour. Immediately after her fall we were called onto the ferry, so we had little choice but to board. Her wrist and arm were painful and swollen, so she took some painkillers. When we docked at Poole we went straight to the hospital, where we found she'd chipped the elbow bone and fractured her wrist. By now I wasn't driving very often because of my heart condition, so we were grateful that we had an automatic, and somehow Lorna managed to drive us back to our home in spite of her injuries.

Lorna's sixtieth birthday was on 15th May, and on this date she had to retire from British Telecom. I think that she was sad in one way to be ending her working life, but the journey and the stress of the job were becoming too much for her, and I was relieved when she retired. Her colleagues gave her a party and many gifts, and we drove back home with her festooned with streamers, carrying her gifts and a bottle of champagne, not knowing whether to laugh or cry.

We'd booked a week's holiday at a cottage in Cardigan, and we spent a relaxing, happy week there. The property was at Neuadd Farm, and there were lovely walks in the countryside, and down to Cwm Tydu, a little cove where we watched dolphins and seals. The weather was very warm and sunny, and I was able to sit and sketch the scenery. I had been warned to keep out of the sunshine, as unfortunately the medication I was taking made my skin sun-sensitive. I thought that I was being very careful to keep out of direct sunlight, but one day whilst I was drawing, the sun moved round and I had my hand and wrist in sunlight for a short while. This made the skin on the whole of my body burn and itch, and we had to go home a day early. I went to the doctor, and discovered that I now had a serious problem. I saw several consultants and tried many different solutions, but nothing seemed to help. We decided to see Dr Thakaram, who was a private consultant. He told me that as I didn't have private health insurance, it would be better for me to return to the National Health Service. Fortunately he also worked in the National Health Service and was able to arrange to see me very quickly at the local hospital. He found I was suffering from dermatitis and eczema, and that part of my problem was due to my dry skin and part was caused by the tablets I was taking for the arrhythmia. This was the start of many years of skin problems, I must have tried every pill and potion available to help this condition, and none of them have been completely satisfactory. The skin consultant arranged for me to see Dr Forsey, a cardiologist at Russell's Hall Hospital, to check if I really needed the tablets that were causing this trouble. Dr Forsey was horrified to learn that I had been on my heart medication since 1992 and had never had a check up. Apparently I should have had blood tests every six months to check for side effects. Now, not only was my skin badly affected, but it had damaged my lungs and was starting to affect my eyes. I was referred to the eye clinic at Dudley Guest, and given another appointment with Dr Forsey a couple of weeks later. I was certainly getting my money's worth from the National Health Service!

My granddaughter Amy had done well with her "A" levels, and had gained a place at Wolverhampton University to read Biomedical Sciences. She went on to get a first class honours degree, and then decided to read medicine at Warwick University. Her younger sister Emma gained a second in Graphic Design at Wolverhampton University. Jean would have been so proud to see the success her beloved grand-daughters were having. It amazes me that my family has had such educational and career choices; it's certainly a far cry from my humble beginnings.

CHAPTER
ELEVEN

After Jean died, in an effort to occupy myself, I joined an art class at Haden House. When I met Lorna I asked her if she could draw, and she replied, "I can't draw a straight line." "I didn't ask you that," I retorted, "Can you write your name?" "Of course I can," she replied very huffily. "Then you're drawing". Once she'd grasped that concept, Lorna grew a little more confident about drawing and painting. She explained that she'd had the same art teacher throughout her school life and had never got on with her, so had given up art as soon as possible. We joined an art class in Dudley, and she was once again responsible for my next invention. She was painting the canal and octagonal lock house at Bratch Lock — a very complicated scene! She asked me how could she do the white glazing bars at the windows, and I passed her a bottle of masking fluid. When we returned home I was horrified to find that she'd used one of my most expensive (and favourite) brushes to apply the masking fluid, and of course it had solidified and ruined the brush. Lorna was unrepentant. She said the masking fluid was too difficult to apply, and that it didn't go finely where she had wanted it. I had to agree with her and decided to make a little gadget to make it easier for her. I spent many hours working in the workshop, and made many failures before I came up with my solution. Masking fluid is a notoriously difficult medium to work with, as it is latex based, but when Lorna tried my answer — a small polyurethene bottle of masking fluid with a fine nylon nib — she was thrilled.

After some consideration, we felt that we might have a viable commercial product, so we christened it the Masquepen and applied for a patent. The next few months were spent perfecting the Masquepen. We found a source for masking fluid and we decided to offer it to the two large art concerns in the United Kingdom, Daler Rowney and Winsor & Newton. They both seemed quite interested, but they kept us dangling for some months, waiting for their reply. Finally they both declined to take the product, which at the time we found disappointing. They both thought it was a good idea but didn't think people would use it. In the light of this we both agreed that we'd forget about marketing the Masquepen, and the following Wednesday saw us back at art class. Lorna had put a Masquepen into her box, and when she was using it her neighbour asked if she could borrow it. Everyone wanted to try it, and our tutor ended up ordering forty! When we got home we talked it over and felt it would be worth trying to market it after all. We designed some labels, and had them printed, and also decided to place a small advertisement in the *Leisure Painter* and *Artist* magazines. This felt such an enormous step, but as we sent off the cheques for a couple of hundred pounds, we consoled ourselves that we could afford to gamble this amount of money. To our delight an artist, Wendy Jelbert, had reviewed the Masquepen in *Leisure Painter*. She had written a very good article praising it and, best of all, had painted a picture demonstrating the use of the Masquepen. Within a day of the magazine going on sale, the orders started flooding in. I don't know what our postman thought, as each day his postbag was full of orders for us! An even bigger shock was in store for us — within a couple of months art shops were ringing us up, telling us that their customers were asking them if they stocked the Masquepen. We then started to supply the shops, gradually running down the mail orders. We found ourselves working full time, making Masquepens, dealing with orders and sending out invoices. We even occasionally had to call in the marines (the family — Rita and Emma) to give us a day's work to keep up with the orders. We had to start ordering our supplies in larger quantities, and the day we ordered two hundred and fifty bottles was such a big day for us.

As if we didn't have enough work, Lorna had decided to work on our family history. She started researching the Cruddas family, and also her own family trees. We were both surprised to find that our ancestors had not originated in Yorkshire, as we had always believed. My Cruddas ancestors had come from Northumberland, and Lorna's had started off in Wales, Suffolk and London! We both quickly got very interested in the unfolding stories, and started taking short trips to Bridlington, Beverley and Newcastle, to meet relatives and to check the archives. Lorna found that the Internet was very useful in our research, and we were able to get back to the 18th century. We are still working on these family histories and still get excited when we find a little more information.

Of course we were still busy with the Black Country Inventors, and I was still making prototypes for new ideas I'd come up with. I invented a small dust catcher for electric drills and sold a thousand to British Telecom. I let this idea drop when someone else patented a very similar idea at the same time. I also invented a flexible carpet gripper which would go round pillars, washbasins, toilets and the like, after watching a carpet fitter having to cut gripper up into little pieces when he was laying a carpet in our bathroom. We went to the Harrogate Carpet Show, but I quickly realised that my idea was a non-starter. However, it wasn't a wasted journey, as Lorna and I enjoyed exploring Harrogate and the surrounding district.

In April 1998 we were asked if we would like to be filmed by Central TV. It was a short item called "Join Our Club". One April day the film crew and our inventors descended on our bungalow. We were all given one or two lines to say whilst demonstrating our inventions, as well as collectively inviting people to "join our club". It sounds very simple, doesn't it — but you'd be surprised at how long it took to film. It was decided that they'd film in our garden, and filming started at about two o'clock. We were all very nervous and it was amazing how many of us forgot or "fluffed" our simple lines as soon as the camera was on us. It was dark and we had to have lights in place to film us by the time the three minutes or so was in the can! A couple of months later some of the members of the Club were asked to appear in the BBC's lunch time programme "Working Lunch". This was filmed at the Black Country Museum and we had a lovely day there. We all discussed our inventions, and the benefits of belonging to the club. We even had a special Drink Station made in Perspex, with Working Lunch details printed on it, and this was also featured on the programme. I have to say that coming out to the car park at the end of filming and finding that some idiot had broken our car's windows and stolen the radio rather spoiled the day.

The only distributor we had found so far for the Pondwand was Oasis, and Lorna and I thought we should try to get them better known. We bought a large map, pinned it on the study wall, and made a circle encompassing twenty miles around our home. We then looked up all retailers of water garden equipment, and spent a day making appointments for our "rep" to call. Over the next couple of weeks Lorna and I drove around keeping our appointments. I think many people were surprised that our reps were senior citizens, but we sold a great many Pondwands. We treated our "sales" days as holidays, taking picnics and having great fun. We were on such a high, and as a result of our calls we found another distributor in Bedfordshire. That summer we were so thrilled when Charlie Dymock from BBC's "Gardner's World" picked out the Pondwand as one of the most useful new products at the Gardeners World show at the National Exhibition Centre in Birmingham. We managed to get a short video of her showing it and telling viewers "it was groovy!" Needless to say it did our Pondwand sales a world of good.

The following May the Black Country Inventors were approached by Putsnams, a large firm of solicitors in Birmingham. They asked if we would like them to sponsor our club for a year. They suggested holding an exhibition of our inventions at their premises in Charles Street, Birmingham. It was a wonderful opportunity for all our inventors to showcase their inventions. We spent the next couple of months preparing their biographies and getting our inventions ready to show. We also invited members of Birmingham Inventors to join us. We then had to send all our paperwork to the public relations firm who were organising the exhibition. The exhibition was scheduled for Thursday and Friday 24th-25th September. We went to Charles Street on the Wednesday to deliver our inventions and set up our stands. We were delighted at how efficiently it had been arranged. There were very professionally printed leaflets and posters, all the stands and display boards we required; they had also organised publicity for the event which was attended by newspaper journalists and reporters and cameramen from ITV and BBC. Throughout the exhibition hot and cold food was served, with wine and soft drinks as well as tea and coffee. It was an inventor's heaven! We all had a terrific time. Lorna and I were interviewed demonstrating the Pondwand in a small pond on the roof terrace for BBC local news. We'd been so successful eradicating blanket weed from our pond at home that we had difficulty finding enough to take with us for the demonstration! We were also filmed demonstrating the Masquepen and Eezetrap (another invention of mine for catching insects) by the BBC and Central Television, and the event was also attended by the Lord Mayor of Birmingham. It was quite an experience, and the club members got a great deal of publicity in the newspapers.

Late on Friday afternoon we had a phone call from Elena, Lorna's youngest daughter, to tell us that her husband Mark had suffered a severe nervous breakdown and was in hospital. She was distraught, so we left Birmingham and drove to Hereford to pick up her and their two young sons, Luke and Jake. They spent the next couple of days with us, and then went back to Hereford, where Elena and Mark had to try to get their lives back together. They found things very tough for several years, but this set-back eventually made their marriage much stronger.

In October, we held another Inventors' Exhibition, this time a weekend show at Merry Hill, Dudley. This was held in the amphitheatre of the shopping centre, and members of the public seemed very interested in the display. After the exhibition was over, we drove to the East Midlands, where we had arranged to have our own pale blue masking fluid produced. We collected twenty-five litres, and were so worried that we might have laid out money which would be wasted. Fortunately sales were still improving, and it wasn't long before the masking fluid was being delivered to us

121

in large quantities. We were approached by three of the major art wholesalers in England, who enquired whether we would supply them wholesale with Masquepens and stop supplying to the shops directly. They each gave us a substantial order, and we realised that we could no longer continue making the Masquepens ourselves. We arranged for the local firm who already made the Pondwand to manufacture the Masquepen for us. Things seemed to be happening fast and furious.

Our local newspaper, the *Express & Star*, had held a competition which Lorna had entered without telling me — and won! The first I knew of it was when I received a letter from the newspaper congratulating me, and telling me that I was one of ten prize-winners who would be attending the New Year's party at the new Millennium Dome. I couldn't believe it, so Lorna showed me her prize-winning entry, where she had told them about my work with inventors and how I had founded the inventors' club. A few weeks later I received the paperwork and the tickets. Each prize-winner was allowed to invite three family guests, so Lorna and I invited my daughter Rita and her husband Robert to accompany us. We were picked up by coach from Dudley on the last day of December, and driven to our hotel in London. There was time for a rest and a meal before getting ourselves ready for the party. The coach picked us up and drove us to the Dome. We could see the illuminated Dome long before we arrived; it was quite thrilling. Security was extremely thorough, and there was quite a delay before we were finally admitted. Once inside we were each given a black cotton bag on which was screenprinted "One Amazing Night!" This contained a souvenir programme, a millennium medal, a quarter bottle of champagne and a plastic champagne glass! Then it was time to tour the Dome, which had many exhibits, all the time being entertained by music, stilt walkers and dancers. Waiters passed around handing out glasses of fruit juice and champagne. I was extremely good and stuck to orange juice, but Lorna and Rita found it very hard to resist the champagne. It seemed that no sooner had they put down an empty glass when a fresh one would be pressed on them. Needless to say, they enjoyed themselves immensely. We were also given cartons containing canapés and delicious little cakes, and then it was time for a thrilling show. We entered the theatre arena, followed by the Queen and Prince Philip, Tony and Cherie Blair, and many other celebrities and worthies. The show opened with acrobatic dancers descending from the top of the dome, and then there was music for all tastes, from Simply Red and Jules Holland to Willard White. At twelve o'clock the Dome was lit up with fireworks, we all joined hands to sing Auld Lang Syne, and then opened our bottles of champagne to toast the New Year. The show ended with very nubile Brazilian samba dancers as well as dancers from the Notting Hill Carnival in the most exotic costumes. At about two o'clock we made our very unsteady and weary way to the coach and returned to our hotel. Next morning, after breakfast we again boarded the coach and returned to Dudley. Needless to say, we were a very weary and subdued bunch during that journey home!

Over the next few months we went on air a couple of times on BBC Radio West Midlands. The first time Lorna and I were interviewed about my inventions. The interviewer, Jenny, was particularly interested in whether Lorna found it difficult being married to an inventor! The second time George and I were interviewed about the club. It was all very interesting.

In July we were invited to visit Art in Action. This is a marvellous craft show which is held in the beautiful grounds of Waterperry House in Oxford each year, and one of our retailers was demonstrating the Masquepen. We drove to Oxford on the Saturday and spent an incredible day there. The weather was warm, and we wandered happily, watching glass-blowers, sculptors, painters, instrument makers, musicians, carvers and many more craftspeople demonstrating their skills. There were marquees where there were demonstrations of paper-restoring, art demonstrations, even story-telling. After an exhausting day we went back to our hotel for a nap, then drove to a restaurant on the River Thames and had a meal under the stars — a wonderful way to end a very special day.

The following weekend we went to London, to visit the Artist & Illustrators Exhibition at Olympia, where once again our Masquepen was being shown. This was another lovely experience; the only thing to dampen our spirits was when Lorna realised that her purse had been stolen on the Underground. There wasn't a great deal of money in it, but all her credit cards, library and phone cards had to be reported and stopped, which was very inconvenient.

For some time Lorna and I had been discussing our roles at the Black Country Inventors. Lorna was very involved in the club doing all the secretarial work as well as being treasurer, and I was still Chairman. We felt that as we were now so busy, it was time to hand over our responsibilities for the club. In March we wrote our resignation letter and the following month we resigned officially at the Annual Meeting. We'd decided that we should attend as many meetings as possible and would still be very involved with the club. After a vote of thanks, Lorna and I were given Life Membership, and the members also bought us two cordon apple trees as a token of their thanks.

I had several more consultations with the cardiologist, Dr Forsey, and in October he explained that he was going to refer me to the Cardiac Unit at Queen Elizabeth's Hospital in Birmingham; and an appointment was made for me with Dr Marshall, who had me admitted. They did a great many tests and discovered that the heart attacks I had suffered over the years had scarred my heart very badly. There was a fairly new technique, cardiac ablation, where the scars are literally burnt off by laser. Dr Marshall explained that if this worked, it could solve all my heart problems. I was told that I would go onto a waiting list and be admitted for this procedure in the near future.

That October was also memorable for another reason — Cruddas Ironcraft closed down after thirty-six years of trading. After my heart attack in 1992

I had given my half of the company to my daughter, and my brother gave his half to his son Graham. Bill semi-retired, and the two cousins ran the business together. Unfortunately, eight years after my retirement sales had plummeted and the receiver had to be called in. I was at a loss to understand why, as when I had retired the company had a very healthy turnover of a quarter of a million pounds and solid assets in the bank. Fortunately we had kept the land separate from the company, so Rita, Graham and his brother Martin were able to benefit from the sale of the land. I was heartbroken at the demise of the company — I had put so much of my life into it. On looking back, I realise that I endangered my marriage and my health to make it successful. Thank goodness I now had such a happy marriage, and that Lorna and I were so busy with Cruddas Innovations that I had little time to mourn my old business.

CHAPTER
TWELVE

In January 2001 we received a call from Michael, the managing director of one of our distributors. He told us he had a customer, David Ford, who was visiting him from the United States. David was very enthusiastic about the Masquepen and wanted to meet us to discuss selling it in the States. We invited them for lunch, and got on extremely well. David was more than enthusiastic, he was so sure that he had a very good new product for America. By the end of the afternoon he was confirmed as our distributor for the States, South America and Canada, and this was the start of a very successful business as well as personal relationship with David.

Towards the end of January I was admitted to Queen Elizabeth's for the ablation procedure. Unfortunately, after the operation we were told that my heart was so badly scarred that they had been unable to do this successfully. This was very disappointing, but Dr Marshall wasn't giving up. He explained that I could be fitted with an implantable cardiac device called a defibrillator. This is a small unit, no bigger than a cigarette lighter, which would be implanted under my skin just below the collar bone. Wires would run inside under my rib-cage into the heart. When my heart beat too fast, the defibrillator would give a series of shocks to slow the beat down. The first shock would be tiny, possibly I wouldn't even notice it, the second would be fiercer, and the third would be very intense. It sounded rather scary, but we all discussed it and we decided that I really had no choice — I had to go for it. Dr Marshall said he would put me forward for the procedure and I could expect to be called back within weeks. Five weeks passed. As we hadn't heard anything, Lorna rang the consultant's secretary. We were rather shocked to be told that out local health authority weren't keen to spend so much money on an operation for me because I was 72 years old. Apparently the operation would cost over thirty thousand pounds, but Dr Forsey assured us he was fighting for me. He said I was very young for my age, still running a business, more active than many of his younger patients, and that he was determined to win. Eventually he did, and I was admitted again to Queen Elizabeth's on Monday 19th March. I had the defibrillator fitted that afternoon, and on Friday, after a pep talk from the technicians and Dr Marshall, a very relieved Lorna took me home. In April my defibrillator fired for the first time. Lorna and I were in bed at the time, entwined in each other's arms, and the shock was fierce enough to send us both to the end of the bed. We went back to the hospital for a check up the following day. The consultant grinned at Lorna and said, "Hello, I hear the earth moved for you too, last night!" The atmosphere was very relaxed, and we were made to feel easy about the occurrence. The technicians adjusted the defibrillator, checked my heart out, and we came home, feeling very much more confident.

The *Express & Star* had been featuring a local financial advisor in the Money page. We decided to call him to review our finances — how we were to regret our decision. He was very affable and appeared very competent. He visited us in August, and we discussed how he could invest our savings more profitably. On the morning of 11th September we drove to his office in Wolverhampton and handed him the cheques he had requested. On our return we decided to have a late lunch — just a quick bite, as it was past our usual lunch time. While we were eating I turned on the television to catch up with the day's news. There was what appeared to be a disaster movie on screen, and we were just about to turn it off when we realised it was live television. It was the terrible disaster in New York. We sat unable to move, almost unable to take it in, as first one aeroplane and then a second crashed into the Twin Towers. Like many other people, we shall never forget that day. A couple of days later we received the financial certificates from our advisor, and were horrified to find they were not what he had led us to expect. We did some frantic telephoning around and fortunately managed to cancel the transactions and get our money back. However, the markets were in turmoil after 9/11, and it took several years for our investments to catch up to their starting point. We very firmly decided that we were our own best financial advisors, and that in future we'd steer clear of the financial fraternity.

In September that year we were contacted by a local artist. He was a graphic designer, who did a great deal of work for Saatchi & Saatchi. He told us he loved the Masquepen, but he really needed a finer nib, and wondered if we could make a one-off version for him. He offered to pay up to one hundred pounds for a suitable nib. I gave the matter a great deal of thought, driving Lorna mad while I considered the problem. I realised that there must be other artists who would find a finer nib useful, and I finally came up with a cost effective solution — and the Supernib was born. We were now selling three Masquepen products, Masquepen, Refill and Supernib, and the distributors were quick to stock the products. David rang us and asked if we could supply the Masquepen products in packs for the American market. They wanted to buy all the products as single items, but also to be able to buy the Masquepen and Supernib packed together, as well as all three items in a pack. We considered this carefully and decided it was a good idea. Lorna had gradually become very proficient on the computer, learning to lay out adverts and leaflets. We were able to design all our own artwork ready for printing, which was a great help. We decided it was now time to design some new instructions, and had these printed in French, German and Spanish, as well as English.

We were getting a bit worried about maintaining the garden and our pool. The garden had a very steep bank, which was becoming difficult for us to weed, and maintaining the lower level was a lot of work. Elena, Mark and their children had come over several times to help us, particularly with maintaining the difficult sloping bank, and one weekend Sara and her family also came to help. Lorna had roses and clematis climbing over the fence, which she loved, but I thought they were getting out of control. I asked Sara to prune them, and she followed my instructions so enthusiastically, that Lorna was following behind her begging, "Oh no, no, Sara, please don't cut so much off!" Sara giggled and kept on cutting, saying she was only following my instructions! One evening I sat down and re-designed the garden to make it easier for us to manage. I decided that we should remove all the flowerbeds from the lower level, have it gravelled, and have a raised pond which would be easier for us to clean. I designed a teardrop shaped raised pond which had a marble slab in the centre. This slab held a fountain and appeared to be floating on the water. I then designed lights that were built into the sides of the pool and illuminated it at night. In order to ensure that everything would work as I had envisaged, I made a full-scale model, something I always do when designing anything.

We got a few quotes and finally settled on a firm called Aquascape. The owner of the company, Richard Bennett, came to measure up and saw the Pondwand hanging by the patio. He was very taken with it and asked if we would sell him the patent and all the rights. We were a little surprised, but when Lorna and I talked it over, we realised it could be good for us. We were now so very busy with the Masquepen that we really hadn't got the time to concentrate on selling the Pondwand.

We agreed to the sale, and by the spring the Pondwand was no longer ours. There have been many times in the ensuing years when we regretted this decision, but at the time it seemed to be the right one.

We had arranged for a member of the inventor's club, John Aston, to check our patents for the Masquepen and the Pondwand. They were just coming to completion, and as John was very experienced with patenting (he was in charge of all patents for a very large international lock company), it made sense for him to ensure our patents were watertight. This was particularly important for the Masquepen as we intended to apply for an American patent. We had already been granted a Trademark for the Masquepen in the United Kingdom, and now applied for the same in America.

The end of the year was very cold with ice and snow so Richard and his workers had great difficulties getting the pond finished as the concrete refused to dry for many days. Finally the pond was done, the ground was prepared and the gravel down. I made some cantilevered steps, so we could get up the bank more easily, and made some stepping stones across the gravel. Once the water in the pond had settled down, we put our fish back in and planted some water lilies. We planted up containers of plants around the pond, and planted up the D-shaped raised bed we had planned at the end of the pool. I'd hidden the electrics for the pumps in a small cupboard on the wall near the pool, so I now made an arch and a mirror to disguise this, and we were very pleased with the results.

132

In May we had an e-mail from Simon (who lives in California) to tell us he was coming home for a visit and would like to meet as many of the family as possible. Simon is my sister Marlene's son and we hadn't seen him for several years. We decided to hold a party for him in June and set about inviting all the family. My cousin Colin and his wife Thelma came from Salisbury to spend a couple of days with us. My daughter and her family, Lorna's daughters and their families, Marlene, both her sons, and my brother Bill and all his family managed to come. The weather was kind to us and we were able to sit out in the garden. Lorna had printed out all the facts she had garnered on the Cruddas family and made up a booklet for each family. We also printed out the family tree and pinned it up in the greenhouse, so there was plenty to talk about.

In July we had a visit from Julie, who'd worked for me at Cruddas Ironcraft for at least ten years. She was now working as a policewoman, and thoroughly enjoying her new job. Lorna and Julie were chatting in the sitting room, when Lorna suddenly felt unwell and collapsed. Julie rang for an ambulance and Lorna was very quickly taken into hospital. I was able to sit with her in Accident & Emergency for three or four hours, when Lorna insisted I went home to have a rest. After I left she was transferred to another hospital, where she stayed for a couple of days. Her blood pressure had been very high, but when it stabilised her medication was changed, and I was able to bring her home. We decided to have a few weeks taking things more easily.

This was easier said than done. We had by now changed our labels for the Masquepen products after consultation with David. In the following Spring I gave some lectures on inventions to the students at Wolverhampton University. Lorna and I were also asked to spend a day with pupils at a local secondary school. We talked to them about invention, and then they were set a challenge to invent and prepare the presentation and an advert for their product. We found it great fun, and the children were very good. It was quite an education to see how the two sexes differed. The boys seemed to argue quite a lot amongst themselves and dithered over their invention. In contrast, the girls very quickly organised themselves, settling on a product and then delegating tasks to different girls!

Lorna had started sending for brochures on Ireland, so I knew I had to go on holiday again. I'm not really a holiday person; I'm always itching to get back to my workshop. We decided to take the ferry from Holyhead to Dublin at the beginning of September. We then drove across Ireland to Galway, staying at different guest houses. It was a very relaxing time, with lovely scenery and very good food. We had been in correspondence with an artist, Liz Audigier, who works during the summer in Ireland. She had asked us to visit her in Clifden if we had time during our trip. We made sure that we had time to see her and enjoyed a very interesting afternoon. She is a very talented artist and demonstrated how she used the Masquepen and Supernib in her paintings. We both enjoyed the trip but

Lorna found the driving very tiring, and we were pleased to get back home. It was becoming very obvious that our efforts to relax were not working very well, and we felt we should give the matter a lot more thought. For one thing, we decided that we would have to cut down on any holidays which involved a lot of driving. Being inveterate list makers, we each began making a list of holidays which appealed to us both.

CHAPTER
THIRTEEN

My skin had been bothering me again whilst I was on holiday, and towards the end of September it was in a very bad way. I had a high temperature, and felt unwell. Luckily I had an appointment with Dr Paul at the City Hospital in September. He told me the skin is the largest organ in the body, and mine was closing down. He refused to let me go home, and insisted on admitting me there and then. I was there for a week, having oil baths, and being covered in steroid cream several times a day. By the end of the week my skin had improved and Lorna was allowed to take me home. She had driven to the City Hospital in Birmingham every day and it was quite a difficult drive for her, so I was very relieved to go home.

We had an order from an art stockist in South Africa in October and Elena and Mark spent a day with us, helping us to pack the order. The following month we had a very large order from Australia, so they came to stay for a working weekend. We were beginning to have concerns about the firm who was currently making our Masquepens and Refills. We were only one of their customers and they were slipping behind with our orders. At this time Mark hadn't got a suitable job, and

Elena was working for Bulmers, the Herefordshire cider makers. All the staff had been threatened with redundancy so she was worried about her future. We suggested that they might like to work full time, making the Masquepen products as a self-employed company, invoicing us for their work. They didn't take long to decide they would love to do this and arranged to take a course with the local Business Link. They set up a partnership Hockham Enterprises, and we helped them with the necessary paper work. They decided to start working from their flat, but were pushed for room and needed to look for suitable premises. We went to see our current manufacturers to explain that we were moving our operation to Hereford, and they were not at all pleased. They refused to let us have our tools back, even though I had provided them all. I quickly started work to duplicate the tools and was even able to improve on the old tooling.

Lorna's daughters were very keen for us to spend Christmas together, so it was decided that we'd go to Hereford on Christmas morning, have lunch with the two families at Sara's house and then spend the evening there, before returning home on Boxing Day. We had a tremendous Christmas Day. Lorna and I were not allowed to lift a finger, and we all had great fun together. It was hectic — Sara and Sam's sons Oscar and Leo were then aged seventeen and twelve; Elena and Mark's sons were aged sixteen and eleven. I don't think we'll ever forget a slightly inebriated Sara prancing through the sitting room with red antlers on her head, chanting "I'm a little reindeer!" Lorna and I were full, quite exhausted, extremely contented, but also very glad to tumble into bed that Christmas night. I only had the one daughter and we didn't seem to spend much time with her family. It seemed strange but very agreeable to be accepted as Grandpa to Lorna's family.

Elena and Mark found a reasonably priced workshop on a farm in Canon Pyon. They agreed the lease and got the keys on the first of January. We went to visit the workshop with them and it appeared to be ideal. We took the new tools over and looked forward to working together. We were initially rather nervous as we didn't know if our sales would carry on being successful, but Elena and Mark told us not to worry. They were so pleased to have the chance to work in their own business, and told us that if necessary they would find some extra packing work. It soon became quite obvious that there was plenty of work for them as the orders continued to flow each month.

In March Lorna's daughters invited us to a Mothering Sunday lunch. We drove to Hereford on Saturday and took some materials to the unit. Afterwards Elena and Mark with their sons Luke and Jake took us for a tour around Hereford Cathedral and the Old House, a medieval house in the centre of High Town which is open to the public. We all went for lunch at the Hungry Horse, then met Sara's family and went for a walk alongside the river Wye, ending up at the Left Bank, a rather new and trendy area of Hereford. We had coffee and cakes there before going to Hedley Lodge where we had booked a room for the night.

Hedley Lodge is in the grounds of Belmont Abbey, which is run by Benedictine monks. We had a wonderful meal and a gentle walk in the idyllic gardens before retiring for a well-earned rest. On Sunday we all met at Sara's house where the girls produced a gourmet lunch for us. We drove back to Quarry Bank in the late afternoon, quite replete, and very impressed with Hereford.

Lorna was still working on the family history projects, and in May we drove to Suffolk. We spent a week at a very luxurious cottage in Eye, explored the countryside and went to the archives to look up Lorna's family. She had a shock to find that her great-great-grandfather had been "baseborn", and we were able to hold the bastardy bond which had been issued upon his birth. The father had been bound to pay the parish council and the mother the sum of sixpence a week each, for upkeep of the child — it was very interesting reading!

6th June will always be remembered as D-Day but that year it was my own personal D-Day. I'd had a very restless night, the smoke alarm started beeping as it needed a new battery, and I had to get up in the early hours to change it. When I got back into bed I couldn't get back to sleep, I had so many things going round in my mind. My main thoughts were that I wasn't getting any younger, and how long would I be able to maintain the bungalow? The garden with its high bank was a challenge, harder to cope with every year. I was also thinking of how much we had enjoyed Hereford and the closeness I had found with the family there. At half past four I woke up my long-suffering wife. "Are you asleep?" I asked. "I was," she replied, "What is it, are you ill?" I pulled back the duvet and passed her a pair of slippers. "No, I'm not, but I've got an idea I want to discuss with you." I put the kettle on and made some tea, and then asked her, "What would you think about moving to Hereford?" She was astonished, but I pointed out that it would be sensible of us to move nearer to Elena and Mark because of the business, and that it also seemed to make sense to be closer to the family as we all got on so well. I wasn't getting any younger, I pointed out, and they were all willing to assist us if we needed help. We drank our tea, and then I got out a large sheet of paper and divided it into two columns, PROS and CONS. It soon became glaringly obvious that there were far more pros than cons; looking back it was astonishing how quickly things fell into place. We contacted a couple of estate agents that same day and made appointments for them to view the bungalow. We instructed one of these agents to sell the bungalow just four days later. The following Saturday, we booked ourselves into a hotel in Hereford for a night and started viewing bungalows. A fortnight later we had accepted a cash offer for our own bungalow and found two very different properties that we both liked in Hereford. After due consideration we settled on a property in Marden, a small but lively village mid-way between Hereford and Leominster, and just twenty-eight days later we had moved in!

As an inventor, a workshop has always been more important to me than a garage, so my car has always stood outside to leave room for my lathe and other tools. I work with many different materials, so collect plastic, wood and different metals, as well as having many prototypes in varying states of completion. One wall was fitted with containers for different sizes of screws, nails, nuts and bolts and other fastenings. The opposite side was used for storing paints, adhesives and other liquids. The family came over several times to help us, and it took us several weeks to pack up the workshop. We ran out of space to store some of the boxes and as the forecast was for dry weather, we put the boxes outside in the garden. Of course, just before we moved, the heavens opened, so when the boxes were moved they were so wet the bottoms collapsed and all the contents fell out! All my organising and labelling was lost as things were hastily thrown into new boxes. It would take me months to re-organise my workshop. We were fortunate to be allowed to have the key to the garage a week early, so we hired a van from Hereford and Elena and Mark picked it up and drove to Quarry Bank. They were unhappy with the van's condition, particularly the brakes which seemed very poor. We loaded the lathe and a lot of the items in, they drove off and we followed behind them. We stopped to have a drink and a chat and discovered they were having a job to control it on the hills — we all drove on with our hearts in our mouths and were so relieved to reach Marden safely.

We had sold the bungalow in Quarry Bank and bought the Hereford property so quickly that we had difficulty in finding a removal firm. We approached all the most reputable and recommended firms, only to find they were all fully booked. We eventually found a small firm, and quickly booked them.

One of our problems was that we just had too much stuff. When Lorna moved in she'd brought a lot of her stuff with her, so we had two kettles, two toasters, duplicate sets of crockery and cutlery, as well as many similar compact discs, so everything had gone up into the loft. As we are both hoarders, there were also many books, ornaments, spare curtains and bedding up there. I've always kept paperwork and we found receipts and papers going back to 1970. This necessitated several days of bonfires in the back garden, as well as hours poring over papers to see if they should be kept. We found my army documents and all my references, and Lorna insisted on reading everything, so it was a very long exercise. Mark came to help us empty the loft and nearly put his back out carrying heavy items down the ladder. For some reason we'd been storing some of Emma and Amy's toys, so these were returned to their rightful owners, and we made many trips to the charity shops. We also attended a boot fair, and sold a lot of unwanted possessions, but both agreed, "Never again". We also both agreed to stop hoarding as we were so surprised at how much we had. We tried to pack systematically, colour-coding boxes according to the rooms they were to go into, and had a book with all the boxes itemised. Alas, plans don't always go according to plan.

On the morning of the removal the vans arrived at seven thirty. The removal men weren't pleased to find quite a lot of materials from the workshop still to be transported and everyone was trying to convince me that I didn't have to bring every little piece of wood, plastic and steel with me! I certainly didn't agree, and later discovered that they were all trying to throw bits away without me seeing. Both the vans were packed by half past ten, we watched them leave, made our farewells first to the neighbours and then to the bungalow, and set out for Hereford. We arrived about half past twelve to find Elena and Mark, Sara and Sam, and Rita, Robert and Emma all waiting at the bungalow, ready to help us move in. We waited, and waited, and . . . waited! We tried to contact the removal firm with no answer. Eventually, at about five o'clock one van turned up with both removal men in it. They'd run out of fuel, then broken down, and finally had to abandon one of the vans on a notoriously steep hill at Clows Top. They'd re-arranged the heaviest things into the larger van and were going to have to go back to rescue the other. As you can imagine, it was chaos. All thoughts of colour coding, or things going into the correct place were forgotten, as we attempted to unload as fast as possible. Rather shame-facedly one of the men asked for an advance on the fee so they could buy fuel! We were all tired and starving, so the women piled into our car and drove to Hereford to buy fish and chips. The second van didn't arrive until after ten o'clock. Sara and Sam had to return home, but the others made up our bed and I made sure the cooker and microwave were working — I certainly didn't want to be hungry the next day! British Telecom had let us down as the promised phone connection hadn't materialised; in fact it was a week before they had us back on line — thank heaven for mobile phones. We eventually fell into bed about midnight, very exhausted, but at least we were in our new home.

We had expected to find tradespeople to make the alterations we envisaged, but as usual, we wanted things done yesterday and we couldn't find anyone free to help us for several months. There was nothing for it but to get down to the work ourselves. We knocked a hole in the wall between the study and the garage to insert a new door, and then made another new door from the garage into the garden. We put down a new tiled floor in the study and set up the desks, bookshelves and computers. The glass in the hall was very dated, so we replaced this with glass blocks. We had the oil-fired central heating boiler taken away, as well as the oil tank in the garden, and put in gas-fired central heating. It only remained to replace the patio doors and make a new deck outside. The existing patio was concrete, and quite dangerous, so I designed a raised deck, which was easy to access from the sun lounge. I had this covered with Astroturf — which I must modestly admit was one of my better ideas. It's so easy to vacuum, and then wash down with a hosepipe — beats mowing the lawn any day! The front garden was bordered by a hedge of leylandii cypress, over a hundred foot long, and a metre deep, with a height of eleven feet. It was very dreary, and we were fortunate to find a landscape firm who removed it all, and left us with a manageable border.

144

We then had the grass dug up and laid gravel, which has made the front garden low-maintenance.

The fireplace wall was covered with wood strip, and there was a huge stone fireplace in the sitting room (very 1960s!) which we hated, so we had a quote to replace the fireplace. We were told it would take a week to remove and cost over three thousand pounds. I can remember kicking the stone fireplace one night, then turning to Lorna and exclaiming, "It can't possibly take a week to remove this. We'll put on the alarm for six o'clock tomorrow and have a go at it ourselves". Next morning we pulled off the panelling and started attacking the stone fireplace. We kept loading the car and driving five miles to the tip to get rid of the rubbish. The car was very heavy, so Lorna had to drive slowly. The men at the tip started to get quite concerned by this pair of old-aged pensioners and we were on first name terms. They very kindly brought over a JCB to unload the stone so we didn't have to lift it. Five trips to the tip and it was all done. We were weary but unbeaten! Next we had a modern hearth and gas fire installed. I went to a local wood yard and bought some Hereford oak with which I made a new mantlepiece and matching side tables for the sofas. I cut out two small circles in the oak, fitted them with blue glass, and placed halogen lights behind the glass. Needless to say our families weren't too impressed by all the work we were doing. We were constantly told that we had moved to find more relaxation, but I was thoroughly enjoying myself.

It only remained to buy new curtains and rugs, and find a new dining-room suite and then the bungalow was to our liking. Elena, Mark and the boys spent Christmas Day with us, and we felt life couldn't get much better than this.

January proved to be very cold and snowy. We were invited to take the Masquepen to Peterborough, where it would be demonstrated on a television craft show. It was a terrible journey, with torrential rain, and we got lost several times finding the studio. The Masquepen item was filmed, but when we left the studio we found the rain had turned to snow, which was driving blizzard-like against the car. I suppose sensible people would have given in and stayed the night, but we persevered and managed to get back to our cosy home. The next day was our wedding anniversary, so as the weather had relented we drove into Hereford and visited the Cathedral. We sat in the Lady Chapel, clasping hands, and quietly renewed our vows to each other. We bought some lobster, put champagne on ice, and had a wonderfully romantic evening — whoever said love was for the young?

In April we had to go back to Dudley to see Dr Forsey who was very pleased with my heart, and we went out for lunch afterwards. As we were in the area, we'd arranged to see Alan, our optometrist, and chose some new glasses. After the long drive home, we both felt very tired and decided to have an early night. In the early hours I awoke feeling disorientated and really ill. Lorna rang the NHS Direct, and was advised to get me to hospital. It was pitch black and raining, but she managed to get me to the car. She had to drive with one hand holding me up. It's a six-mile journey to our hospital in Hereford, but Lorna says it felt like twenty miles. I was eventually admitted, and after a battery of tests found to be suffering from blood poisoning. I hadn't realised how ill I was, and to my disgust I was to remain in hospital for three weeks. The family split visiting into three shifts. Lorna visited in the daytime; Sara, who works as a receptionist in the Accident and Emergency department, visited me in her lunch breaks; and Elena and family came at night. Of course, being me, I made a certain amount of protest and was finally allowed out on parole on Good Friday, with a proviso that I went back each day for an intravenous dose of antibiotic, and that I return to my hospital bed on the following Tuesday. Fortunately the infection was soon under control, and I was allowed back home a few days later.

Elena and Mark felt it was now time to sell their flat and move on to a house. They discussed it with us and we felt it would be a good step for them to take. They found a small terraced house in Hereford and thought that they would be able to work from there, so gave up the lease on their workshop. The sale went through quite easily, and by August they were settled into their new abode and very contented to be working from home. It saved them a good deal of travelling as they were now nearer to Jake's school and the shops, as well as being closer to us.

In January we had very sad news from my nephew Graham. His father, my brother Bill, had died the night before. Bill and his wife Peggy had been in Wolverhampton, to see a show at the theatre. They'd decided to have a cup of tea before the show when Bill suddenly collapsed and died of a heart attack. It was such a shock as Bill had no record of heart disease. We attended his funeral a week later and I was filled with regrets that we had grown less close over time. Of course, our move to Hereford had put more miles between us, and I find it very sad that we didn't get the chance to enjoy more time together in our retirement years.

Lorna and I decided that now we were well settled into our new home it was time to have a good holiday, and thought it would be a good idea to try a cruise. We booked a week on the P & O cruise ship *Oriana*, visiting France, Spain and Portugal. I was rather worried that I should be bored, but was surprised to find that there were so many things to do that I was kept quite occupied. This short break was useful, as it gave Elena and Mark a taste of being responsible for the business whilst we were away, and Lorna had finally found a holiday which I couldn't cut short to get back to my workshop — well, not without swimming! She informed me that the following year we should think of booking a longer cruise, and promptly sent for brochures.

We were still busy with the Masquepen sales, and received orders from Canada, Holland and Thailand in addition to our normal sales. We decided, on our accountant's advice, to change the partnership into a limited company and were pleased to find that our patent for the Masquepen had been granted in the United States.

One Saturday morning in late November I received quite a severe shock from my defibrillator; in fact it knocked me to the floor. Lorna rang the Queen Elizabeth hospital in Birmingham, and they advised her to make me rest and keep an eye on me. In the afternoon it occurred again, and she was told to take me straight to the local hospital, where I was checked over. They weren't used to defibrillators, and Lorna was a bit surprised when they showed her a print-out of my heart tracing and asked her, "Does this look like his usual tracing, do you know?" She explained that she hadn't ever seen one before, and they scratched their heads and said they couldn't find anything obviously wrong, and allowed me to go home. The next day we went for a short walk in the village, when I collapsed once more, falling into the road. Neighbours rushed to help, I was very unsteady on my feet and desperately hoped they didn't think I was inebriated! This time I was admitted to the cardiac ward, and on Monday morning I was taken by ambulance to Birmingham. Lorna drove there and was waiting for me at the ambulance entrance. After very thorough checks, it was found that the wire going into my heart had fractured, and that I would need an operation to remove it and insert a new wire. A bed was booked for December 15th, and we went home with instructions to "take things easy". The doctor had arranged for Lorna to sleep at the hospital accommodation, and so on the 14th we packed our bags and drove once more to

Birmingham. The surgeon talked to us both the night before the operation, and told us that it was going to be rather difficult and that he had to warn us that the possible outcome could be bad. I asked what my options were, and he replied, "There aren't any." Well, that settled it, and I told him I should have to go ahead. We both had a restless night. Lorna came to sit with me before I went to the theatre, and the nurses told her to go and have some breakfast and try to relax.

She was sitting reading when one of the technicians came up to her and gave her a hug. "He's fine," she was told, "He's in recovery, and doing very well" There were a few tears before Lorna came back to the ward to wait for me, feeling that once again her prayers had been answered. The following day she was able to drive me home — I don't think I was ever so relieved to see our garden and bungalow. Lorna hadn't made any Christmas preparations, so the next few days were spent writing Christmas cards, shopping for food, buying and wrapping presents. The decorations were hurriedly put up, and the tree decorated. The families came to visit at Christmas but only stayed a short time so Lorna and I could have a quiet time together. The snow fell soft and gently on Christmas Day, and we sat, arms about each other, drinking a glass of champagne and thanking God for the Christmas we both thought might not happen.

CHAPTER
FOURTEEN

Since moving to Hereford it's become the tradition for Elena and Mark to give us lunch to celebrate my birthday. They have an old monk's chair, which they always make me sit on at the head of the table, on a golden cushion. There are always birthday banners on the walls, and the table specially laid with flowers, candles and crackers. The family always produce a special beautifully illustrated menu for me. The last one was:

Inventors Delight
Seafood starter of scallops and prawns in tempura batter

A Yorkshireman's Special
Roast Beef
Yorkshire pudding
Elena's special roast potatoes
Baby carrots, broccoli and Mediterranean vegetables

Grandad's Grumble
Home-made apple crumble with custard or ice cream
Coffee
Home-made chocolates and petits fours

Now who could resist a menu like that? Jake usually spends some time preparing games such as charades for us to play, or perhaps Trivial Pursuit, before we take ourselves back home, feeling very cherished. When he was ten, Jake had begged his parents for a dog, promising that he would be responsible for its care. Eventually they had given in and let him choose a "rescue" dog from the RSPCA. His choice was Ollie, a Jack Russell cross, who for some reason can't leave me alone. As soon as he hears our car, he's waiting for me at the front door. He cavalierly ignores Lorna and I have to ignore everyone else and play with him until he quietens down. If Lorna visits the family without me he looks very puzzled, and keeps walking past her and looking hopefully at the front door. Lorna tells me that we really should have a dog too, but I feel that at our time of life they are too great a responsibility, so I shall just enjoy Ollie.

Lorna was still working on the family histories, and in the following January she had an e-mail from a lady in North Carolina, U.S.A. One of her neighbours, Leonard Barnes, was also doing his family history, and she had shown him Lorna's request for any information about her great-great-grandfather, William Bryn, who she believed had gone to America in the 1850s. William was also Leonard's great-grandfather, and he knew a great deal of the family history. He phoned us one Sunday evening, and told us that he was 99 years old, living alone, still looking after himself and still driving! He sent Lorna all the paper work on her family, and we were fascinated to learn that William and his bride Jane had travelled from Wales to America in 1851, where he had a contract to lay railway lines. Three children had been born to them. In May 1857 in Arkansas, they joined a wagon train which was going to California. Unfortunately, when they reached Utah, the wagon train was attacked by Indians and the Mormons. Everyone on the convoy over the age of ten was killed. Lorna's great-grandfather Thomas and Leonard's grandmother Ann were some of the twenty or so children who survived. They were rescued by a cavalry officer and taken back to Arkansas. Somehow, we don't know how, they were taken back to their grandparents in Wales. Leonard was fascinating to talk to, and so very lively, and kept in touch with us by phone and letter. He celebrated his hundredth birthday with a big party in his small town of Gerton, which almost everyone attended. His congressman presented him with a card from the President, and when he was presented with a flag that had flown over the White House, he was so thrilled.

In May we went on another Mediterranean cruise, this time on the *Sea Princess*. Lorna had managed to convince me that two weeks was a reasonable time from home, and after some initial resistance I agreed. We went to Monaco, Barcelona, Florence, Rome, Sardinia and Gibraltar. We enjoyed the trips, the food, the shows and the company, and I even got used to all the dressing up. I've always enjoyed dressing casually and complained bitterly about having to wear not only a jacket and tie, but also a dinner suit. However my wife informed me that "I scrubbed up beautifully, and just to enjoy it", so of course I did. I wish sometimes that I could dance as Lorna really enjoys dancing, but even she admits that I've got two left feet and doesn't try to get me on the dance floor. We made full use of the Cyber Lounge, reading our e-mails and keeping in touch with the family. We received an order from Japan and realised that, thanks to modern technology, we could still manage to run the business successfully. Much as I enjoyed the cruise, I was pleased to get back to Hereford; I really am a home bird!

We had a phone call from David, our distributor in the States, telling us that he was in Europe with his family and that he would make a flying visit to Hereford towards the end of July. He drove to visit us, and after a chat we took him to the Left Bank where we met Elena, Mark and Jake. We sat in the sunshine, overlooking the River Wye, and discussed the Masquepen products and how the business was going in America and Canada. It was useful for David to meet the family, and for him to see how they were developing within the business. We are pleasantly surprised at the speed with which the Masquepen has established itself on the other side of the Atlantic — not bad going for a pair of senior citizens!

After the panic of last Christmas, when we didn't really know if I'd be alive to celebrate it, we enjoyed preparing for this year's festivities. Lorna made home-crafted cards (using the Masquepen, of course!) and it was decided that we would host Christmas Day lunch. Our guests were Elena, Mark, Jake, Luke and his girlfriend, Sara, Sam and their son Leo, and we had a wonderful time together. It was all the more precious for our scare the previous year. Lorna and I made up our minds that we would live each day as if it was our last, savouring every moment together. We really do feel very blessed, and so fortunate to have found this late-flowering love.

As soon as Christmas was over, we decided to plan our final cruise. I really felt that I would enjoy one more, but that would be enough for me. We decided to travel at the end of May on the *Queen Mary* to New York, spend five days there, and then travel back to Southampton again on the *Queen Mary*. I had previously been to America with my first wife Jean, and I wanted to visit there again, this time with Lorna. The *Queen Mary* is such a luxurious vessel; the trip to New York was sheer delight. All the family had been worried about my boredom threshold; after all this time we wouldn't be stopping off to explore a new country every couple of days; we'd be at sea solidly for six days. Lorna threatened that if I played up she'd send me down to the engine room for the whole voyage — whatever made her think that would be a punishment? There were wonderful stage shows each night, and usually a film or performance each afternoon. We visited the only Planetarium at sea, and also attended three or four lectures. The food was delicious, and one morning we went to a show given by two of the chefs, demonstrating their signature dishes. We docked at the new cruiser berth on Sunday morning, disembarked, and got a taxi to our hotel.

After the luxury of the voyage, our time in New York was rather a disappointment. Our hotel left a lot to be desired, it was on Upper East Side and involved quite a lot of walking to get to the hub of the city. The weather was quite cold and wet, and to cap it all, Lorna developed phlebitis on both legs. Fortunately antibiotics kept it under control, but it made getting about New York very difficult. On our penultimate day David flew from San Francisco to meet us, and we had lunch in the famous Algonquin Hotel. Lorna loves reading, so she was thrilled to be in the place frequented by Dorothy Parker and Robert Benchley. That day it had poured down, and when we reached our hotel we were cold and soaking wet. Unfortunately, as far as the hotel was concerned it was summer, so there was no heating and nowhere to dry our clothes. We had a hot shower, and cheered ourselves up by remembering that the next day would see us back on the *Queen Mary*. David came to our hotel in the evening and we had dinner in the rooftop restaurant. The view from the terrace was really spectacular and we all enjoyed our meal. Next morning we picked up a cab to take us to the ship. The taxi drivers in New York don't have "the knowledge" like the London cabbies. Our driver was clueless and had no idea how to find the new berth at Brooklyn. We stopped whilst he asked policemen, firemen, passers-by — we could see the funnels and the words *Queen Mary* 2 in stainless steel on her superstructure — but he still couldn't get us there. We started to giggle; it looked as if we would spend the day touring Brooklyn! We were very pleased to finally embark again on the *Queen*

Mary. We soon settled back into the routine of the ship, met the friends we had made on the outward voyage and before we knew it, we were back in Southampton.

Lorna's eldest grandson Oscar and his partner Kelly had a baby girl, Faith, just before we sailed for New York. I teased Lorna about having to sleep with a great-grandmother — it didn't seem quite so funny when she reminded me that I was now a great-grandfather!

As soon as we were home we were occupied again with the business. The Masquepen was still doing very well, with many repeat orders as well as new ones from Korea. I had two small innovations for which I had made prototypes but never tried to promote. One of these was the Eezetrap, a tool for catching spiders, insects and butterflies at arm's reach (Lorna hates spiders, and won't go near them) and the other was the Rotasharp, which cleans and sharpens rotary electric razor heads. Now I had some spare time, I made up a few of each, and Lorna put them up on e-bay. They started selling very quickly, and before long I had to spend part of each day in the workshop to keep up with the orders. Lorna and I have occasionally discussed slowing down, but I'm pleased to say that an American gerontologist we met on the cruise advised us to keep on working as long as we feel fit. I've got at least 39 ideas on the computer, if I feel like working on a new innovation, and at least one more invention is at prototype stage. Hopefully Elena and Mark will take a more active role in the business as we do relax more, and I am sure they will continue to make a success of it.

We're very proud of our children, they are all doing well, and our grandchildren are a delight. Amy graduated from Wolverhampton University with a First, then went to Warwick University to read Medicine and will be graduating soon as a doctor; Emma also went to university, got a good degree in Graphic Design, and is pursuing her career; Oscar and his partner are now parents, caring for their baby daughter Faith; Luke, after a difficult start, has developed into a strong, happy young man his parents are proud of; Leo is about to start an apprenticeship in Joinery; and Jake is doing extremely well at school, and expects to go on to university. Antony's children are much younger. Sebastian is a very bright boy, who's just started school, and Eleanor is a lively toddler.

We now intend to enjoy every moment we have and to squeeze every bit we can out of our remaining time together. We very rarely argue, as our tastes are so similar. The one thing we do occasionally fall out over is my desire to always organise everything to the "nth" degree. Lorna says if I try to organise her any more, she'll meet herself coming back! I am trying very hard to be more laid-back, and Lorna delights in getting me out of my comfort zone! In the words of one of our favourite songs, "Love is wasted on the young", and I believe it is; I certainly know love gets more intense when one knows time is limited. We are now busy making lists of things we want to do. We feel so fortunate to be so much in love, and so happy in our life together. So what does the future hold? I'll be 78 next January — perhaps more inventions — another business — a self build bungalow — who knows? There might even be a sequel to this book!

LORNA'S VIEWPOINT

I've told Len's story more or less as he told it to me. The first chapters were quite hard going, as Len can remember every (sometimes boring to my female mind!) detail about power stations, steel mills and wrought iron, but finds it difficult to remember personal details — especially those that hurt. I have been lucky that Rita and Peggy have helped me to "see" Jean, and I also felt her very close to me in the early days of my marriage to Len. It was quite strange that whenever I was polishing the grandfather clock in the corner of the sitting room I'd feel her so near to me that I would talk to her, and thank her for making Len such a marvellous husband; or sometimes, when he was being more pedantic than usual, to grumble, and ask her if he'd occasionally driven her mad! When I mentioned this to Rita, she said, "I'm not surprised that you feel her there, that clock was her pride and joy."

I met and married my first husband, José, when I was eighteen — never was the old adage "marry in haste, repent at leisure" more apt. José was Portuguese, and there was a tremendous difference in our culture and outlook. As far as he was concerned, women were second-class citizens, and wives, in particular, should know their place. He had a vile temper and would strike out, or throw things in rage, and I soon learned to give in to him, just to keep the peace. We had a daughter Elizabeth, who died in an accident when she was three and a half; a son Antony; a still-born son; another daughter Sara; a little girl Luisa who died at three weeks; and finally another daughter Elena. We struggled to make the marriage work as he was a womaniser, and in fact I brought up his illegitimate daughter (also called Elizabeth) from the age of ten to eighteen. It was only the fact that we had children to bring up which kept me committed to the marriage.

Somehow we managed 27 years, finally running a business together, and with time things seemed to have settled down. In November 1985, however, he went on a business trip to Brazil and failed to return! It was a great shock, and I felt totally lost. The children and I were left to run the business, and it was an even greater shock to find that he had enlisted the help of our bank manager (who was his personal friend) to ensure that I sold the business and sent him half the proceeds. The bank manager insisted that the money from the business was sent to him before fees and taxes were paid, so I had to find those out of the money I had left, which made a great difference to the way I could live. Fortunately we found a reasonable house in Worcester, and I managed to find a job with British Telecom.

For several years I concentrated on getting a home together, and being with my family and my grandchildren. Then around 1991, I decided it was time I found a life for myself. I joined Worcester Hospital Radio, where I eventually had two programmes a week; then I was asked to become the Union Treasurer at work, and a few months later I joined a social club called Nexus. This was the best move I could ever have made; I made so many friends and enjoyed coffee evenings, walks, the theatre, dinner parties and short holidays. The most important thing that happened to me was that I found how to laugh again — I really think I'd forgotten how to enjoy myself — and even to be silly on occasion! My particular friends were Glenda, Pat, Sue and Rosemary. We were all either widowed or had been left by our husbands, and we all tried to make the others laugh and to forget the bad times. Although Nexus wasn't a dating agency, several people met and married new partners directly or indirectly through the club. Glenda met her husband Barry, who was a member of the Worcester group; Pat met her husband Tony, who belonged to the Birmingham group, and I met Len through Ken, who was a member of our group.

When Ken suggested that Len and I should meet I was very dubious. I'm so glad that I eventually said yes. When Len rang me on the Thursday night I was busy packing to go on holiday with Glenda. The year before Glenda and I had been to Scotland for a holiday; now we were going to a cottage in North Yorkshire for a week. Len was soft-spoken, and we quickly found we had a lot in common. We were surprised that we were both from "God's country", and the more we talked, the easier it became. There were no awkward pauses; it was as if we already knew each other. Len was also leaving for a week's holiday the next day, and asked if I would like to meet for lunch when we both got back. I agreed, and he arranged to pick me up at twelve o'clock the day after our return. I shared the house with my youngest daughter, Elena, and her partner Mark, and discussed it with them. I started getting "cold feet" about meeting a stranger and Mark offered to lend me his mobile phone, in case I felt I needed help! Glenda and I had a lovely holiday, and she told me that she was seeing Barry and that it was looking serious. She'd been so badly hurt when her first husband had left her for his personal assistant, so it was lovely to see her having a chance of happiness again. On our third day in Yorkshire, Barry surprised us by turning up unexpectedly, and he stayed with us for a couple of days, driving us to various places such as Bolton Abbey and Castle Howard. It was marvellous to see them so happy together, and they tried very hard not to make me feel left out, but I suppose it did make me feel lonelier than ever.

When Len phoned me on our return I agreed to meet him, and he picked me up the next day. My family had recommended that we had lunch at the Fox in Bransford, so that's where we went. Right from the start there was no uneasiness, we chatted like friends, telling each other about our lives. After lunch, Len suggested that I should show him Worcester, so we parked behind the Cathedral and I gave him a guided tour. We had tea at the café in the Cloisters, and afterwards went for a walk. As we crossed the road Len held my hand, and then continued to hold it, and it felt so right. We walked and talked, and talked and walked; it was hours later that Len eventually took me home and asked me to see him again. My family were waiting anxiously to hear how I'd fared, and I was able to tell them that I'd had a wonderful day, and that we were going to meet again.

Our next meeting was the Nexus treasure hunt. We had a marvellous day together and I eventually returned with Len to the bungalow to "see his snooker room"! We played a little snooker, had several cups of tea, and then Len made us a light meal. It was getting quite late, so he suggested that I stayed the night — he even offered to sleep on the sofa! I phoned my daughter to let her know I was staying, and was quite reprimanded, "Mum," she asked "What are you doing? You hardly know this man, you'd have been furious if I'd behaved like this." I had to smile, and she carried on, "We've been so worried about you, I'm glad you remembered to phone, we've been sitting up waiting for you." I calmed her down, feeling more like a naughty teenager rather than a 54-year old mother. The next morning Len drove me back to Kidderminster to pick up my car, and I popped home before going to the office. My daughter and son in law still hadn't really forgiven me. Mark asked me, "Why do you think phones were invented, Mum? You should have rung us much earlier, we were worried about you driving in the dark," and once again they succeeded in making me feel like a naughty little girl. I was glad to escape to work!

Len invited me to spend the following weekend with him. I drove from Worcester, and as I entered the bungalow he was playing Jim Reeves singing "Welcome to my World!" — that was very romantic! On Saturday night I cooked a meal for us, and was surprised to find he hadn't got a wooden spoon. I must have made a fuss because a few days later the postman delivered a slim Perspex tube containing one perfect red rose — and a wooden spoon! In no time at all we were a couple, and one of the most surprising things I discovered was that Len valued my opinion, and included me in choosing things, such as bedside lights or new coffee tables. This was such a change from my previous marriage, where my husband made all the purchases from the smallest pieces of furniture to cars, and even our first home, with no reference to me. I do really find it hard to understand how we bonded so quickly, it seemed as if we had always known each other. We used to say that we must have met in a previous existence as there were so many strange coincidences, and half-remembered memories. Even some parts of our lives had been quite similar. Our parents came from Yorkshire, our mothers had both been in service, Len's mother had two boys and then a girl in her early forties; my mother had two girls and then a boy at the same age, and both of those late siblings had been rather spoilt. Our mothers were both very hard workers, and both, for different reasons, had been disappointed in the men they had married.

The only fly in the ointment, as far as I was concerned, was Len's brief marriage to Pam. Somehow it really worried me. I saw photos of her, she looked so glamorous, and as he found it difficult to talk about her, I couldn't see why the marriage had failed. I wondered how I could compete, and if he'd think he'd made a mistake in choosing me? The breakdown of my marriage had left me with very low self-esteem, and a lack of confidence. I had gradually built up a façade of confidence, but that was all it was, a façade. However, Rita and Len's mother both talked to me about my worries and told me that my relationship with him was different, more solid, a quite different situation. They both explained how lost he was after Jean's death, and how he had snatched at a new chance of happiness without ensuring that they were truly compatible.

Len was so pleased that his family had managed to convince me that we had a future together. Of course, at first there were some minor difficulties, as there are in any new relationship. Having been left to make a new life for myself, I'd held down a job, drove a car, could change a fuse, put up a shelf (all right, you couldn't actually put anything on it!), and Len had been used to a very traditional wife, who stayed at home and looked after the house. He was the one who had done everything else, and he found it very difficult at first coping with such an independent woman. On the other hand, I often found Len very set in his ways, needing routine and organisation in his life. My friends used to laughingly state that my untidiness would drive him insane, but somehow we've merged our personalities — he's made me more organised and I've managed to occasionally shake him out of his rut. He says if we're in a rut, it's one we've designed together.

Neither of us could ever have foreseen how our lives would develop over the coming years. Who could ever have imagined that Len's inventions would cause us to start up firstly a partnership, then a limited company, and that we would be selling our products all over the world? We've made friends with people in America, Australia, New Zealand and Holland though our Masquepen sales. It's very unlikely we'll ever meet them, but we keep up a lively correspondence thanks to the Internet. One of our regular writers is Miggles, or Margaret to use her given name. She calls me Podge, my childhood nickname, and we send each other long letters about our lives, as well as chatting about painting, gardening and our families. Miggles often sends me funny jokes as well as some very inspirational e-mails, and I make sure that I forward these to my friends and family. Len has encouraged me to work on my own interests, particularly on our family histories. I've traced the Cruddas name back to the Border Reivers. These Border Reivers were fighters in the 16th century, fighting the English in skilled guerrilla warfare on the Scottish/English boundaries. I tease him that looting, pillaging and raping are part of the family history, but he tells me he's not up to the raping these days!

I've been amazed by the breadth of Len's ideas; his thoughts and ideas are very often astounding. I can say, "Why can't I?" or "Why is this so difficult?", and very quickly he'll come up with a solution to my problem. Of course, that's the definition of an invention — an answer to a need — and he always says I provide the need! There's occasionally a drawback. He has in the past come up with these solutions whilst I've been at work — and I've been very surprised by some of them! Our fridge in the old bungalow was in the corner of the kitchen, and being small and fat, I often found it difficult to reach to the back of the fridge. One hot summer morning I took out a carton of yoghurt, only to find it out of date, and when I came home that evening Len proudly directed me to the fridge. I found he'd removed all the shelves and replaced them with Perspex rotary shelves. It was really a very good idea, but one had to be very careful not to spin them too fast or food would be propelled across the kitchen; it also meant that there was limited space for large items, such as joints, but it was definitely a talking point amongst my friends!

Another bonus we've found is the joy of having my children and grandchildren living nearby. We see Elena and Mark regularly as we work closely, but also see Sara and her family frequently. Tony, with his second wife Melanie, and their two children Sebastian and Eleanor live further away, so unfortunately we don't get together very often. We do enjoy the company of our grandchildren. We all feel so blessed that the grandchildren have such a wonderful grandfather; he is a marvellous role model for them. Len is very much the typical Yorkshire man — blunt (sometimes too much for many people's sensibilities), hard-headed, and sensible, yet underneath this façade, a tender, caring and romantic person. I hope I've done justice to Len's story; he really is such a very special man.

A FEW WORDS ON INVENTION

Many inventors are convinced that their invention will make them very rich. Some inventors do hit the jackpot: look at James Dyson and Trevor Baylis for example; but it's not easy. There are many pitfalls for a would-be innovator to navigate. We always say that "ideas are the easy part" and that the key to success is marketing.

If you do have a good idea, first of all, keep it to yourself until you have done your research. Try searching the Patent Office's database to see if your idea is original. Fortunately these days it's easy to do this on the Internet. If you're satisfied that it is new, then apply for your patent. It doesn't cost anything to apply for it, and if you can't afford a Patent Agent, there is plenty of help around to aid you in making your own application. The Patent Office will send you a pack with all the information you need to do this. When I applied for my first patent for the Pondwand, Lorna and I pored over the instructions for several days. We spent some time writing out our patent before printing it and sending it away. There is a time lag between the application and the examination, which gives you the protection to try to sell or promote your invention. At the time of examination, you might find, as we did, that it pays to let a Patent Agent check it over and answer any questions from the Examiner. Be prepared to spend some money on this, but you will have saved a great deal by doing the preliminary work yourself. If you can afford it, or don't have the confidence to do it yourself, bring in a Patent Agent at the start.

If you *are* a budding inventor, please steer clear of companies who offer to "help" you with your ideas. We've investigated some of these, and have found them at best to be a waste of money; at worst that they can really rip you off. There are quite a few useful books which we've enjoyed. Some of these are:

- *The Business of Invention* by Peter Bissell & Graham Barker
- *How to make money from ideas and inventions* by R Rogers
- *The Practical Guide for people with a new idea* by Laurence Shaw

Do try to find an Inventors' Club. As a member you'll get unbiased advice, help, and the benefit of your fellow-inventors' experience. Don't be blinded by your own invention, listen to the impartial advice from fellow inventors rather than friends and family! Know when to let go of an idea — sometimes one just knows an invention is not going to take off for one reason or another, and that's the time to move on.

Invention is a fascinating subject and anyone can have a good idea. We always say that ideas are the easy part; it's the production and the marketing that are more difficult! Don't let that put you off though, and do try to have more than one project simmering. I find if I get stuck with one idea, I move on to another until inspiration strikes again. One of our friends in the Black Country Inventors Club always says, "Necessity may be the mother of invention, but poverty is the father!"

Good Luck!
Conceive — Believe — Achieve

USEFUL LINKS

- **Black Country Inventors**:
- The contact is:
- Chairman: John Aston
  www.bcic.org.uk
  e-mail: invent@bcic.org.uk

- **Birmingham Inventors**:
- The contact is:
  Hon.Chairman: Richard Brosch
  www.birmingham-inventors.org.uk/
  e-mail: inventors@lymore.com

- **Malvern Inventors**
  www.malvern-inventors.co.uk
  e-mail: info@malverninventors.co.uk

- **The Patent Office**
  The Patent Office
  Concept House
  Cardiff Road
  Newport
  South Wales
  NP10 8QQ
  01633 814000.
  www.patent.gov.uk
  E-mail: enquiries@patent.gov.uk
  You'll find the staff there extremely helpful — and patient!

- **The Institute of Patentees and Inventors**
  www.invent.org.uk
  E-mail: ipi@invent.org.uk

- **The Federation of Small Businesses**
  www.fsb.org.uk www.cipa.org.uk
  e-mail: mail@cipa.org.uk

- **The Chartered Institute of Patent Attorneys**
  www.cipa.org.uk
  e-mail: mail@cipa.org.uk

- **Wessex Round Table of Inventors**
  www.wrti.org.uk
  e-mail: membership@wrti.co.uk

MY INVENTIONS

The first invention I made after Lorna and I were together was the **Popparoll**. This gadget holds two toilet rolls tidily and discreetly in the bathroom or cloakroom. It is either freestanding, or can be hung on the wall.

We tried rather half-heartedly to market this, but eventually just made enough in my workshop for friends and family.

Another of my innovations was the **Strawberry Stand**. This stand made it easy to hold pots of strawberries, high enough to water and harvest. I had automatic watering and feeding, and had the feet standing in small pots, topped up with beer, which kept slugs and snails off the fruit! There was also provision for netting to stop the birds helping themselves!

The **Pondwand** was a very useful invention. The blanket weed was gathered on to the "wand", the handle then slid down, pushing off the blanket weed into a neat sausage. We sold this at watergarden centres locally before selling it wholesale to distributors. Although we sold this patent, the buyers let the patent lapse. We made a few modifications, and re-applied for a patent. This Spring we have just started selling them again!

The **Eezetrap** was my solution to Lorna's horror of spiders. There is a three foot handle, so she doesn't have to go close to the insect, a ring is pulled and the spider is trapped inside the plastic trap, which is then held closed for disposal. This is also very useful for moths, wasps, bees, butterflies and the like, as the soft brush pushes them into the trap without harming the insect.

The **Eezehand** was another of those good ideas which I didn't pursue, as I found someone else had patented a very similar gadget. I made this after my stay in hospital, where I was told to apply cream to my back several times a day. I was lucky to have Lorna to do this for me, but I realised that there were a lot of people living alone, who could find this difficult. The Eezehand had a curved handle with a disposable pad.

The **Rotasharp** is one of those very simple ideas born of necessity. The heads on my rotary electric shaver needed replacing, and I found they would cost nearly as much as a new razor! I bought a new one, then (being a thrifty Yorkshireman) I stripped down the heads from the old razor and found a way of re-sharpening them.

The **Masquepen** has been our biggest commercial success. We started selling it in December 1995, and we now sell the Masquepen, Refill and Supernib. The Masquepen has a 0.8mm nylon nib, and the Supernib has a 0.4mm stainless steel nib. Although we originally developed it solely for use with watercolour, once it sold into the United States, many other uses were found for it. It's now used for watercolours, acrylics, glass etching, scrap-booking, altered pages, and many other applications we'd never even thought of!

The Masquepen products are sold throughout the U.K, U.S.A, Canada, Australia, South Korea, Japan and Europe.

The **Drink Station** was another little innovation I came up with to help Lorna. She had an unfortunate habit of spilling coffee at her desk! This high-walled, weighted coaster holds her drink safely. This was another item we didn't pursue commercially, but has been a useful gadget for ourselves and friends.

I always tell inventors to write down their ideas straight away. I always have at least forty ideas on my computer. They aren't always practical at the time I think of them, or they need more thought or information. However, having them saved on the computer means that I can always look at them and see if anything new comes to mind.

Some of the ideas on the computer which could be worked on in the future are:

- A flexible, curved carpet gripper — useful for fitting carpets around toilets, loos, pillars
- A new type of slug trap
- A different type of pooper scoop
- Protection against purse snatchers
- Protection for handbags in cars
- A new type of drinking cup for invalids
- Intruder deterrent
- Spectacles finder

Sometimes an invention is put to one side because I have found someone has already patented something too similar. This was the case with the Eezehand and the Caretaker. I invented the Caretaker after Lorna had spent a day with an engineer, watching how he worked as part of her job at B.T. She mentioned to me that engineers had to be very careful not to damage furnishings with brick dust when drilling holes at customers' homes. The Caretaker is an envelope, pre-printed with a template showing the drilling holes, with a low tack backing. It's placed where the drilling is to take place; the dust goes into the envelope, which can then be thrown away. We had an initial large order from B.T, and although this wasn't taken any further, because someone else had produced a plastic model, we still made a profit.

I made a joke miniature version of the Pondwand for a friend who was a young chef. He'd suggested a small version would be useful for serving spaghetti, so I made him a small tool in stainless steel, based on the Pondwand, called the Sperver!

It's great to be able to play with ideas and gadgets. I hope I can keep doing this as long as possible — it certainly beats daytime television!

SOME OF OUR FAVOURITE WORDS

We're a very sentimental pair, and these are some words
we both enjoy.

Grow old along with me!
The best is yet to be,
The last of life for which the first was made;
Our times are in his hand
Who saith "A whole I planned,
Youth shows but half; trust God: see all, nor
be afraid".

From *Rabbi Ben Ezra* by Robert Browning

A book of verses underneath the Bough,
A jug of wine, a loaf of bread — and Thou
Beside me, singing in the Wilderness —
Oh, Wilderness were Paradise enow!

From *The Rubaiyat of Omar Khayyam* translated by
Edward Fitzgerald